THE FRENCH COOK

THE FRENCH COOK

SAUCES

HOLLY HERRICK

Photographs By Steven Rothfeld

GIBBS SMITH
TO ENRICH AND INSPIRE HUMANKIND

"La bonne cuisine est la base du veritable bonheur."

(Good food is the foundation of true happiness.)

—Auguste Escoffier

First Edition
13 14 15 16 17   10 9 8 7 6 5 4 3 2 1

Published by
Gibbs Smith
P.O. Box 667
Layton, Utah 84041

1.800.835.4993 orders
www.gibbs-smith.com

Design by Sheryl Dickert
Page production by Melissa Dymock
Printed and bound in China

Gibbs Smith books are printed on either recycled, 100% post-consumer
waste, FSC-certified papers or on paper produced from sustainable PEFC-
certified forest/controlled wood source. Learn more at www.pefc.org.

Library of Congress Cataloging-in-Publication Data

Herrick, Holly.
The French cook : sauces / Holly Herrick ;
photographs by Steven Rothfeld. — First Edition.
pages cm
title: Sauces
Includes index.
ISBN 978-1-4236-3238-2
1. Cooking, French. 2. Sauces. 3. Cookbooks. lcgft I. Rothfeld,
Steven, photographer. II. Title. III. Title: Sauces.
TX719.H39 2013
641.5944—dc23
2012033320

To all French chefs everywhere, including my chefs and mentors at Le Cordon Bleu, especially Jean Claude Boucheret. *Merci a vous!* You all make the world a more beautiful and delicious place.

Contents

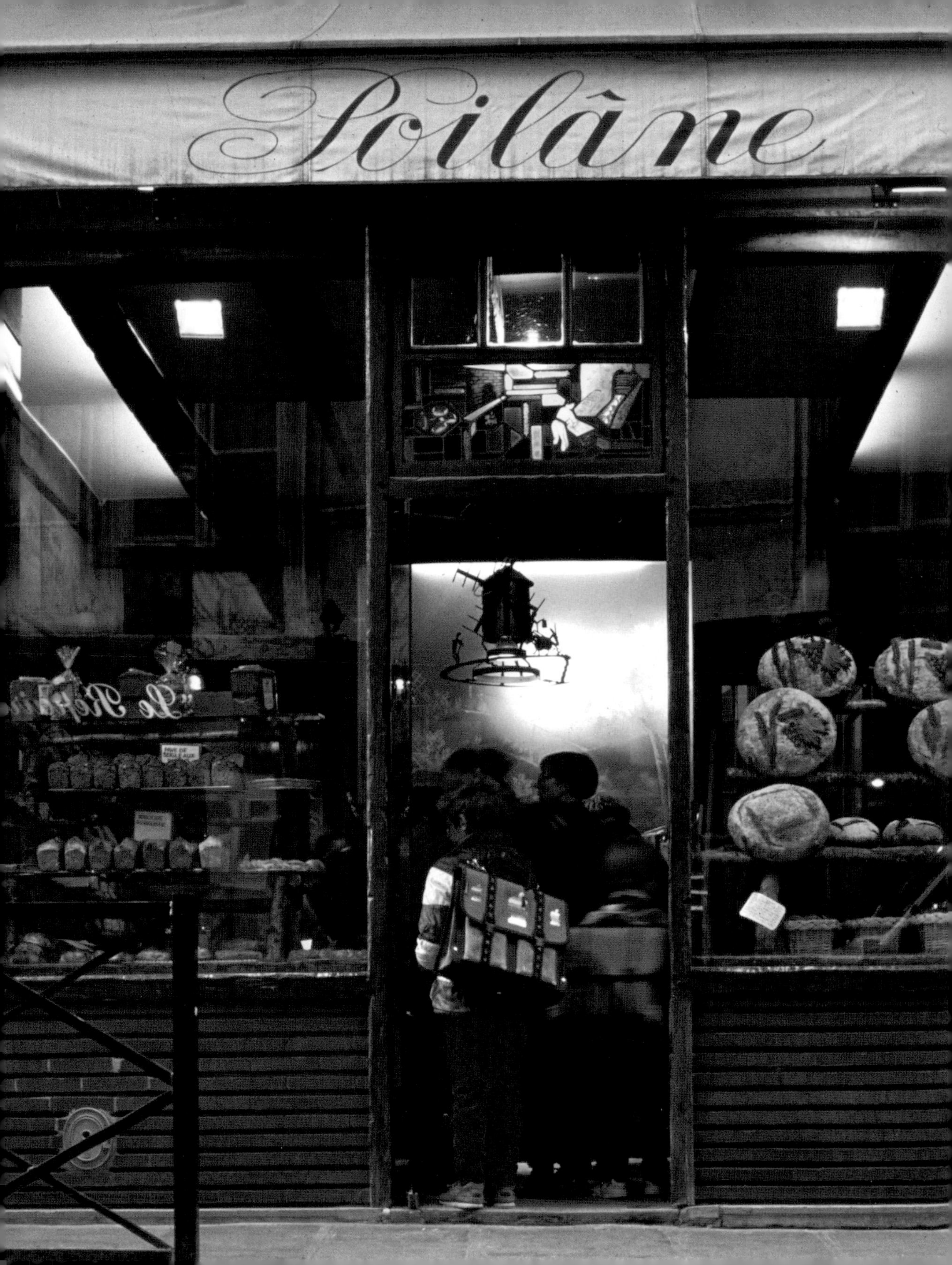
Poilâne

INTRODUCTION

As a new bride in the 1990s, uprooted from New York to another state, I had time to indulge my interest in cooking, long-held since childhood and cooking with my nanna. Relying very heavily on *The Way to Cook,* by Julia Child, which had been a wedding present, I immersed myself into the wonderful world of (mostly) classical French cooking. I was quickly hooked, simmering and saucing and roasting my way towards all kinds of new foods and pleasures.

The cooking itch soon became a passion, and that's just about when all of the really lucky confluences started happening. I decided to put my college journalism major to work not in general writing, but in food writing in particular. My mother-in-law, a marvelous cook and an ardent gourmand, went along with my husband and me to my first-ever food and wine festival in Aspen, Colorado. It was there that I saw Julia Child, my childhood idol, performing a demonstration in which she tackled a rather large steamed lobster with a huge mallet. I summoned the nerve to approach Julia and ask what she thought I should do to get qualified as a food writer. Her graceful answer was actually more of a question: "Can you get to Le Cordon Bleu in Paris?"

I practically squealed *oui!* As good fortune would have it, my husband supported me on this quest. Many years of having studied French and functioning as a sort of uninitiated Francophile practically carried me over the ocean to Paris. Upon landing, a sense of clarity and purpose hit me in a flash, even as I saw the little rabbits scurrying around the fields surrounding Charles de Gaulle airport. I was home, and it felt *delicieux.*

In France, I learned that a beautifully executed sauce is integral to every dish with which it is served. Since then, I've worked in many kitchens and traveled all over the world, but nothing has touched me like my French experience, and, in my mind, classical French sauces still reign supreme.

Here are a series of short cooking lessons on how to turn out classic sauces like the French do, to deftly tackle a Hollandaise or virtually caress the goodness out of and into a silky Sauce Suprême. Beautiful sauces can help make a meal a masterpiece, and they are so much fun to make.

It's an honor to be the author of this first volume in The French Cook series.

If it's fair to equate the ethereal, sensual qualities of food and cooking to those of music, I assert that where the main ingredient is the tune, sauce is the harmony. In a great sauce, all of the elements play with the essence, marrying them in a concert of flavor.

In France, *sauciers* (sauce chefs) are some of the most revered masters in professional kitchens. They are respected for their knowledge and creation of nuance, and also because they oversee the making of some of France's most adored creations—*les sauces*. In a land where bread exists as much to sponge up every last bit of delicious sauce as to spread with butter, sauces rule.

The evolution of sauces from rudimentary purees of bread and broth for dressing meats and vegetables really began in the kitchens of royals, long prior to the French Revolution in 1791. In post-revolutionary France, the stream of kings' chefs and their collective culinary knowledge trickled down to the burgeoning restaurant industry now catering to the public. This parade was largely led by celebrated *maître de la haute cuisine* Marie-Antoine Carême.

But it would be another great French chef, Auguste Escoffier, who would ultimately streamline the work of Carême and others into classical categories and techniques in his many works, including his celebrated and comprehensive cookbook and reference book *Le Guide Culinaire.* Affectionately known as "the king of chefs and chef of kings," Escoffier, is credited with classifying the five classical French mother sauces: *velouté, espagnole, hollandaise, béchamel,* and *tomate.* Each of these mother sauces has myriad derivative "small sauces," which, with the addition of various well-paired ingredients, are designed to suit particular foods. The exact ingredients and at what point they're added have been modified over time in many professional kitchens. These master recipes are not set in stone, but the basic formulas have remained essentially the same.

The French Cook—Sauces is by no means intended to be a complete book of all French sauces, but each chapter provides an introduction to one of these mother sauces, with distinctive recipes that employ some of the flavor layering and building so inherent in classical French sauce-making. In addition, I include a chapter on basic stocks and *fumets* (foo-MAYs), the bases used in so many of the classic sauces, plus a chapter on mayonnaise. (Though not classified as a mother sauce per se, mayonnaise is pervasive in French kitchens and very versatile.)

The art of making divine sauces is not difficult but demands both technique and instinct. Taking shortcuts usually produces limited flavor rewards. Because so many of these sauces require a series of reductions, the balance of quantity and quality of salt is important. Use sea salt, kosher, or another organic salt, avoiding those that contain bitter preservatives or chemicals. Finding the balance of seasonings (salt and pepper) requires careful tasting along the way. I suggest at what point to add them but do not specify exact amounts. Also, since some foods commonly used in the French kitchen are either difficult to find or prohibitively pricey in the United States—e.g., veal and truffles—I suggest alternatives.

While testing and writing recipes for this book, often with a series of small pots simmering, reducing and steaming away, I frequently felt equal parts chemist and magician. The final results were, according to my group of taste-testers, "magical." I hope you'll get a few smiles and enjoy learning the techniques you will need to create your own sauce magic. Bon appetit!

Équipements pour la Préparation des Sauces
Equipment for Preparing Sauces

China cap—This is a cone-shaped strainer with small holes. It is used to do the initial straining of stocks and some sauces to remove any solid matter or stray bits such as bones and vegetables. Its name is derived from the shape of the hats worn by the Chinese. Available online and at specialty gourmet shops.

Chinois—Similar to a China cap, this is probably the most important piece of equipment in a sauce kitchen. It has a longer cone shape than a China cap and an extremely fine sieve. It is used to remove the larger solids that made it through the first pass of the China cap, and is used for sauces, stocks, custards, and more to help ensure a flawless, silky texture. Available online and at specialty gourmet shops.

Ladle—A deep, broad ladle is essential for skimming stocks and sauces and also to help guide the liquid through both a China cap and a chinois, through gentle swirling and pressing motions.

Whisk—A whisk is a must-have in a sauce kitchen, particularly for mounting emulsion sauces, like mayonnaise, or whisking butter into a hollandaise. A medium-size, narrow whisk will do the trick. No balloon whisk *necessaire!*

Best-quality roasting pan—For achieving a nice golden color on the bones and vegetables to create flavor and color in brown sauces, a roasting pan is helpful. Teflon-coated pans won't do the job. I recommend a heavy-bottomed, stainless steel roasting pan, ideally with a copper bottom for even heat distribution.

Stock pot—For the home kitchen, a good-quality 8- to 12-quart stock pot should do the trick. The sides are straight and tall to help regulate tempered evaporation and reduction. An 8-quart Dutch oven will also give good results, though the sides are not as tall or straight as on a stock pot.

Saucepans—A collection of small, medium, and large straight-sided saucepans (*casseroles*) will facilitate refrigerator storage of sauces, reheating and putting finishing touches on warm sauces. This collection should also include at least one slope-sided saucepan (*sauteuse evasee*) for preparing warm emulsions such as hollandaise and béarnaise. Look for best-quality stainless steel with a copper bottom for even heat convection.

Stacked mixing bowls—These are an added bonus in any kitchen and are handy when straining stocks or mounting emulsion sauces such as hollandaise and mayonnaise. Nonreactive bowls such as glass work best.

Food processor—Food processors, though not mandatory, are a huge aid in the sauce kitchen for making quick work of mounting emulsion sauces and puréeing others.

Good-quality knives—All kitchens should be equipped with at least a paring knife and an 8-to-12-inch chef's knife. For cutting up bones and stocks, the latter will work, but a really heavy, nice-quality cleaver is even better. Keep them sharp.

Cheesecloth—It is helpful, though not necessary by any measure, to have this finely woven cloth at the ready. Lining a China cap or chinois with cheesecloth will ensure that not a single solid tidbit—such as a peppercorn or a shred of a vegetable aromat—makes its way into a silky, elegant sauce such as velouté.

WHEN IN PARIS, DEHILLERIN IS A MUST-DO

Julia Child famously shopped here and to this day, it's where many of Paris's most celebrated chefs do their culinary equipment shopping. Tucked away in a corner on Rue Coquilliere 18–20, near les Halles, it is a veritable treasure trove of cooking accouterments.

Slightly musty with a 200-year-old patina, the shop has shelves reaching from floor to ceiling, featuring copper casseroles, chinoises, a battery of knives for every possible job, and so much more. Consummately Parisian, the staff leans towards being brusque, but they'll service your every need, especially when a smile and an effort at speaking French are on display. Don't miss it if you're in the City of Light. Pictures and more information are available at www.e-dehillerin.fr.

CHAPTER 1

LES FONDS
Stocks

Fonds, or stocks, are the starting point for many sauces (though not all; for example, hollandaise and béchamel rarely use them). Because stock is often the first and last layer of many classic sauces, it's crucial that stock quality be top notch—(rich in flavor and color), especially when reduced, as it so often is (see Sauces Prepared with Stocks and Reduction Sauces, page 105). As with anything in the kitchen, if you begin and end with something sub-par, chances are pretty good your sauce (or soup) will be, too.

Stocks derive their flavor from the most basic of ingredients—bones, vegetables, crustacean shells, meat, or a combination of some of these—simmered gently together. Stock variations included here are:

Brown stock—made with browned beef or veal bones and classic vegetable aromats (ingredients that add aroma and flavor, classically, onion, leek, carrots, and celery).

White veal stock—prepared with veal bones and classic vegetable aromats, but the bones and vegetables are not browned. It is often used in white and cream-based sauces such as béchamel and velouté to enhance flavor.

Chicken stock—made with skin-on chicken meat, chicken bones, and classic vegetable aromats.

Vegetable stock—typically made with classic vegetable aromats onion and sometimes leftover bits of other mild vegetables, such as mushrooms.

Fumet—fish stock made with fish bones, heads, tails, and classic vegetable aromats, minus the carrots.

Court-bouillon—a quickly cooked broth prepared with classic vegetable aromats that serves as a poaching liquid for meat or fish. The bouillon is later reduced and finished as a sauce.

Demi-glace—any kind of stock—white or brown, typically using veal, chicken, pork, or beef—reduced down to a glaze (to about 20 percent of its original volume) and later reconstituted in various sauces.

Glace de crustace—or crustacean stock, made with crustacean shells, such as shrimp, crab, lobster, or crayfish that is cooked with classic vegetable aromats and cooked down to a glaze (about 20 percent of its original volume). It is whisked into sauces for garnishing crustaceans or fish to concentrate the crustacean flavor.

Techniques for the different kinds of stock vary, but the theme is basically the same—producing maximum flavor and gelatin extraction (if bones are used) with minimal ingredients. It's also another very practical way to avoid waste (which is a *très français* frugal notion), by putting to good use otherwise unsexy by-products from the kitchen.

The idea with stocks is to make them into subtle, flavor-layered versions of their name. For example, a beef stock should taste and smell intensely of beef, with subtle whispers of the vegetables and herbs with which it is cooked. Typically, the core vegetable aromats of classical French cooking include onion, carrots (though not in a fish stock), leeks, celery, maybe a bit of garlic, plus a *bouquet garni* (herb bundle) of thyme, parsley, and bay leaves. The ratio of vegetables to bones and cooking liquid needs to be respected in every stock you prepare. Even though stocks are useful for using up odds and ends, if you end up throwing two pounds of tired carrots into a stock prepared with two pounds of beef marrow bones and beef scraps, your "beef" stock will end up tasting more like tired carrot soup. Which, as one of my instructors at Le Cordon Bleu used to say, *"n'est pas bon!"*

In restaurant kitchens, long-cooked stocks (such as beef or veal) are often put on to cook at an extremely low simmer overnight and unattended, to be strained and skimmed the following morning for use in the kitchen later in the day. You can try this method at home, but I like being there to oversee the entire production, and perhaps more importantly, to inhale the splendid aromas. Also, the skimming of fat and protein as it forms in a simmering stock is crucial to its flavor and visual clarity (more on this in brown stocks, pages 22–23).

Most stocks store very well in the refrigerator for several days or freezer for several months, with the exception of a *fumet*, which should be used the day it is made. Storing in one- or two-cup containers makes using the stocks later more convenient.

While some very good stocks are available and will do in a pinch (see suggested alternatives on page 28), it's impossible to believe that the grade of ingredients is as high as it would be if made at home. And the inclusion of chemicals and excess sodium can really clobber the flavor of a good sauce, especially one involving a reduced stock. But the biggest satisfaction in making homemade stock is the process—cathartic, sensual, slow, and so aromatic. You can't get that in a box!

Let's take a closer look at each type of stock and how to make it the very best it can possibly be—as a launching pad for many stellar sauces.

Les Fonds Brun— Bœuf et Veau

Brown Stocks—Beef and Veal

Beef and veal are arguably the most crucial sauce foundation stocks because they're so widely used, and they are prepared exactly the same way. The only difference is that the former uses beef bones and the latter uses veal bones. It's important for flavor reasons to get a little meat in there too. Because veal can be expensive to purchase and hard to find, I recommend using a combination of some of the cheapest, most flavorful, and most accessible cuts. For beef stock, I like a combination of beef marrowbones and bone-in beef short ribs. For veal stock, I find that shanks work best. For either, if they're not already cut into 2- to 3-inch-thick disks, ask your butcher to do the job. The more exposure the pan has to the marrow and bones, the more gelatin will be released to add desired viscosity to the stock. There is no reason to get fussy about perfectly shaped, petite vegetable cuts. These will cook for a very long time; so chunky is desirable, lest they cook down and into the stock, rendering it a kind of undesirable vegetable soup. Also, they will ultimately be discarded, so no one will see them.

The first step—very important—is to get the bones and vegetables a nice golden brown. This can be done on the stovetop in a stock pot, but I find the best results begin in a roasting pan on top of the stove (using two burners) and finish in a hot oven. After that, the roasting pan is deglazed with wine and finished with water before the long cooking process (5 to 8 hours) begins on the stovetop in a stock pot.

It's tempting to season a stock, but classically, stocks are not seasoned at all, because they are often reduced (concentrating flavor), so the seasoning is done at the time the sauce is being prepared and finished. I break from tradition slightly in my kitchen and suggest you do the same. A tiny pinch of salt and a dash of black pepper form a nice flavor jumpstart in the early cooking process and browning of the bones and meat.

Skimming—When beef or veal stock first comes to a boil before being reduced to a simmer, the proteins and fats from the meat and bones will begin to rise to the surface in the form of froth or foam. This needs to be removed or it will re-absorb into the stock, causing a cloudy, murky bitterness. Leave a small bowl half full of fresh water and a shallow ladle near your stock pot. When foam comes up, dip the ladle just under the surface of the foam, skim it off, and return the ladle to the water bowl. Repeat several times in the first half hour of cooking, and later, about every 30 minutes. Do be careful not to skim too deeply below the layer of the scum or you will be removing valuable stock.

After this, it's a patient waiting game, as the stock just barely simmers (avoid boiling altogether after the initial boil), emitting its gorgeous aromas along the way. This is a great time to grab a good book and enjoy your fragrant handiwork.

Finish the stock by straining through a China cap and then a chinois (extremely fine mesh). Refrigerate shortly after preparation; it will store very well for a few days in the refrigerator or months in the freezer. Discard the vegetables or add to the compost pile. Pull the delightfully braised and tender meat from the bone and toss it in a steak sauce to prepare a simple Sloppy Joe mixture. (Marrowbones do not splinter and are canine-friendly, but be careful not to share the very small ones, as a dog may choke on them.)

FOND DE BŒUF
Beef Stock
(MAKES ABOUT 8 TO 10 CUPS)

The roasting of the bones and veggies renders this versatile, fragrant stock the rich color of roasted chestnuts. Skimming, slow simmering, and straining ensure beautiful clarity and deep beef flavor that will enhance any beef or meat-friendly sauce.

2 tablespoons olive oil

2 tablespoons unsalted butter

2 pounds beef marrowbones, cut into 2-inch-thick rounds

1 1/2 pounds bone-in beef short ribs, coarsely chopped

Tiny pinch of sea salt or kosher salt

Pinch of freshly ground black pepper

1 large onion, quartered

2 large ribs celery, cut into 2-inch lengths

1 large leek, white part cut into 2-inch lengths

2 carrots, peeled and cut into 2-inch lengths

2 tablespoons tomato paste

1 cup full-bodied red wine (e.g., a Merlot or Cabernet Sauvignon)

14 cups cold water (or just enough to barely cover the bones and vegetables)

3 garlic cloves, peeled

1 bouquet garni (several sprigs fresh thyme, fresh parsley, and 2 bay leaves)

5 peppercorns

Preheat oven to 500 degrees F.

In a large, sturdy, nonstick roasting pan, heat olive oil and butter over medium-high heat (using two burners if necessary) until bubbling vigorously. Add the marrowbones and short ribs. Season with salt and pepper. Brown, turning every few minutes to color all sides, cooking a total of about 10 minutes. Add the onion, celery, leek, and carrots, and toss to coat. Place the roasting pan on the middle rack of the preheated oven. Roast for 10 to 15 minutes, tossing once or twice to turn. Add the tomato paste, stirring well to coat the bones and vegetables evenly. Let cook 5 to 10 minutes more. (*Note*: This is an important step to cook out the acidity of the paste).

Remove roasting pan from the oven. Return to the stovetop, with the burner(s) set on high. Deglaze the roasting pan with the red wine, stirring with a flat-edged wooden spoon to scrape up any brown bits. Cook until the wine has reduced by half.

Carefully, turn out the all of the contents of the roasting pan into an 8- to 12-quart stock pot. Add the water, garlic, bouquet garni, and peppercorns.

Bring to a boil, then reduce to a barely discernible simmer (water barely moving). Skim initial froth and foam carefully with a ladle and discard. Repeat 2 or 3 times during the first 30 minutes of cooking, then every 30 minutes. Cook for 5 to 8 hours, or until the stock has developed a rich flavor and color and reduced by about one-third. Carefully strain the stock through a China cap over another large pot or bowl, setting the solids aside. Strain a second time, through a chinois. Store in airtight containers in the refrigerator for up to 3 to 4 days or in the freezer for several months.

CLEANING LEEKS

The delicate, subtle onion flavor of leeks is sublime, but cleansing their interior layers of frequent grit takes some attention. Trim away the root end and very top of the green part. Remove any frayed or dirty exterior layers. Cut a 2-inch-deep X into the top green end. Pry open and run this end under the faucet, pulling to loosen and remove any grit. For added measure, rest the cut, cleaned leek X side down in a glass or bowl of clean, cool water before using.

FOND DE VEAU, BRUN
Brown Veal Stock
(MAKES ABOUT 8 TO 10 CUPS)

Use the same recipe as for the beef stock, but substitute 3 pounds veal shanks for the beef marrowbones and short ribs.

FOND DE POULET
Chicken Stock

(MAKES ABOUT 8 TO 10 CUPS)

Though better quality commercial chicken stocks are more ubiquitous than veal and beef, making your own is going to ensure the quality and produce the olfactory and gustatory pleasure of preparing it. I recommend starting with a whole 3- to 4-pound chicken. Rinse it, pat it dry, and cut it into smaller pieces with a sharp cleaver or chef's knife. The easiest way to approach the job is to cut the breasts away from the spine and ribs, then cut each in two; separate the legs from the carcass and cut each in two. Finally, hack at the ribs and spine to break it up into a few pieces. The goal is to expose cut bone to maximize flavor and gelatin content in the stock. If you don't feel comfortable doing this, ask the butcher to, or buy pre-cut meat with the skin on.

After straining the solids from the stock, save the meat off the bones for chicken salad or soup. The stock should be fragrant and a clear, pale yellow color. Unlike the veal and beef stock recipes, chicken bones and veggies are just very lightly browned.

2 tablespoons olive oil

2 tablespoons unsalted butter

1 (3- to 4-pound) whole chicken, cut up into 8 pieces

Tiny pinch of sea salt or kosher salt

Freshly ground black pepper

1 large onion, quartered

2 carrots, peeled and cut into 2-inch -lengths

2 large celery ribs, trimmed and cut into 2-inch lengths

1 large leek, cleaned (see Cleaning Leeks, page 23) and cut into 2-inch lengths

3 garlic cloves, peeled

1 bouquet garni (sprigs fresh thyme, fresh parsley, and 2 bay leaves)

1/2 cup good-quality white wine (e.g., Pinot Grigio or Chardonnay)

14–16 cups cold water (just enough to barely cover the chicken and vegetables)

5 peppercorns

Heat together the olive oil and butter in an 8- to 10-quart stock pot on the stovetop over medium-high heat. When bubbling, add the cut-up chicken. Season very lightly with salt and pepper. Sauté lightly, stirring once or twice, for about 5 minutes. Add the onion, carrots, celery, and leek, stirring to coat. Sauté lightly for an additional 2 minutes. Add the garlic, bouquet garni, and white wine. Increase heat to high and reduce the wine by half. Add the water and peppercorns.

Bring to a boil, then reduce heat to a barely discernible simmer. Skim the initial layer of foam with a ladle and discard. Repeat 2 or 3 times during the first 30 minutes of cooking, then every 30 minutes. Cook uncovered for 3 to 4 hours, or until liquid is reduced by about one third.

Carefully strain the stock through a China cap over another large pot or bowl, setting the solids aside. Repeat a second time through a chinois. Store in airtight containers in the refrigerator up to 3 to 4 days or in the freezer for several months.

Fond de Veau, Blond
White Veal Stock

(MAKES ABOUT 8 TO 10 CUPS)

Used in some white sauces, such as béchamel and velouté, the goal is to extract the flavor of the veal and vegetables without "coloring" the sauce through browning, roasting, etc. Prepare it the same way as the chicken stock, except substitute 2 pounds veal shank or marrowbones for the whole chicken.

NOT JUST FOR SAUCES

In the same way that beautiful homemade stocks help form the layers of flavor in outstanding sauces, they can be put to use in soups. After you make a batch for the freezer, use any extra to prepare a fast, nutritious, and tasty soup. Sautéed onions, leeks, and carrots simmered together with chicken broth, leftover roasted chicken, with noodles added 10 or 15 minutes before eating, makes a speedy chicken soup dinner. Or do the same with mushrooms and ground beef topped off with beef stock and barley for a hearty winter feast.

FUMET DE POISSON
Fish Stock

(MAKES ABOUT 6 CUPS)

Fish stock is relatively quick-cooking, coming together in just 20 minutes. Make it the day you're going to use it, as it loses freshness fast. Look for bones and heads from white fish such as haddock and cod. Salmon and tuna are not good picks, since they can make the stock bitter. I don't use carrots in fish stock, as they can muddle the color.

$2^1/_2$ pounds fish heads and bones
$1^1/_4$ cup best-quality dry white wine
   (e.g., Chardonnay or Pinot Grigio)
1 onion, thinly sliced
1 leek, thinly sliced

1 bouquet garni (fresh thyme, fresh parsley,
   and 2 bay leaves)
Tiny pinch of sea salt or kosher salt
6 cups water

Combine all of the ingredients in an 8-quart Dutch oven, stock pot, or large, deep skillet. Bring to a boil and reduce to a simmer, skimming initial and subsequent foam from the top, cooking for 20 minutes. Strain through a China cap first, then through a chinois. Reserve warm or in the refrigerator until ready to use.

COURT BOUILLON

(MAKES ABOUT 5 CUPS)

Court bouillon is a wine- and vegetable-fortified quick stock for poaching another ingredient, frequently fish or chicken. The bouillon flavors the poached items, while they give a second layer of flavor to the bouillon as they cook. Frequently the remaining broth is reduced, or thickened, and prepared into an accompanying sauce. This is best done just a moment ahead of time and used immediately.

2¹/₂ cups best-quality dry white wine (e.g., Chardonnay or Pinot Grigio)

1 onion, thinly sliced

1 rib celery, thinly sliced

1 carrot, peeled and thinly sliced

1 large bay leaf

5 whole peppercorns

Tiny pinch of sea salt or kosher salt

2 cups water

Combine all of the ingredients in a large, deep skillet, bring to a simmer, and cook for 10 to 12 minutes. Reserve for use in the next step of the recipe.

THOUGHTS ON DEMI-GLACE

All stocks, including brown beef and veal as well as chicken and crustacean, can be reduced to a demi-glace, or half-glaze stage. In brown sauces, the process involves starting with the stock, combining it with an espagnole sauce (see Sauces Prepared with Stocks and Reduction Sauces, page 105), and reducing down roughly 80 percent of the total liquid, which then is a glace. Because it's exceptionally time-consuming and expensive to do the former, I'm a huge proponent of simply using the stock in question, and either reducing it down as I'm preparing the sauce, or thickening it with a *beurre manié*—a paste prepared with equal parts butter and flour.

Additionally, there are many fine prepared brand-name glaces available. Here are some of my favorites:

Veal Demi-Glace: D'Artagnan makes an exceptional prepared veal demi-glace and also is an excellent source for other hard-to-find French specialty items, from truffles to duck fat. www.dartagnan.com.

Assorted demi-glaces and bouillons (including low-sodium and vegetarian alternatives): Better Than Bouillon has a vast assortment of flavors, all top quality. They are easily accessed at www.soupsonline.com. Search for the Better Than Bouillon brand product line at this site. I recommend, in particular, their chicken, beef, and seafood demi-glace products. The added bonus is they store well in the refrigerator for extensive periods of time after opening.

GLACE CRUSTACÉS
Shellfish Fumet/Glaze

(MAKES ABOUT 1 CUP)

Shellfish, especially shrimp, crab, and lobster, house a huge amount of flavor in their shells. In a shellfish fumet, the shells are crushed and seasoned with wine and vegetables, cooked down for a few hours to extract flavor, strained, and then later used to finish as a sauce. I like to reduce this stock all the way down to a glace, or glaze. It stores longer, and the flavor is ultra-condensed and rich. Buy the shrimp with the shells on, remove the shells (reserving the shrimp flesh for another use), and pop the shells into the stock pot. Stone crab claws are relatively inexpensive, and the meat inside adds big bonus flavor.

1 tablespoon olive oil

1 tablespoon butter

1 leek, finely chopped

1 celery rib, finely chopped

1 pound (roughly 4) stone crab claws, crushed

Shells from 1 pound fresh shrimp (reserve shrimp
  for another use)

1/2 cup best-quality dry white wine

8 cups water

1 bay leaf

Tiny pinch of sea salt or kosher salt

In a large saucepan over medium heat, melt the olive oil and butter. Add the leek and celery, tossing to coat; cook until just softened, about 5 minutes. Pound the crab claws with a mallet or heavy pot to crack and partially crush the shells. Add these, along with the interior meat, and shrimp shells to the pot. Stir to coat. Cook briefly, then increase heat to high. Add the wine, stirring, and cook until it is reduced down to basically nothing. Add the water, bay leaf, and salt. Increase heat to medium to produce a gentle simmer, skimming off the initial and latter foam, and continuing to skim at 15-minute intervals during the cooking process. When the fumet is reduced by half, strain with a China cap. (*Note*: You can stop here, if you like, for a fumet. Freeze or refrigerate as you would a stock). To reduce it to a glace, return the strained liquid to a clean pan and keep cooking until it gets very concentrated and "glaze"-like. You should have about 1 cup left. Strain through a chinois and refrigerate for several days or freeze for several months.

CHAPTER 2

La Belle Béchamel
Basic, Beautiful Béchamel

Of all of the classical French mother sauces, *béchamel* (pronounced BESH-ah-mel) is the simplest and most basic. There really is not much to preparing it. The sauce begins with a white roux composed of equal parts flour and butter plus a bit of shallot or onion. It is finished with milk or cream, ultimately forming a thickened, milky, mellow sauce. And that's where the beauty begins. The simple flavor backdrop invites myriad additions, from herbs to cheese, as in a Mornay (page 36). Béchamel is also the glorious glue that holds together gratins, lasagnas, casseroles, and even that good old American classic mac 'n' cheese.

A béchamel sauce comes together in less than 10 minutes and can either be incorporated immediately into a recipe or stored in the refrigerator for up to 3 days. Reheat it gently, whisking the entire time, before using. A basic béchamel also reheats nicely in the microwave on low heat.

There are just a few things to keep in mind while preparing a béchamel. First, for a roux, the flour and butter are always in equal parts.

The butter goes in first and then is joined by a finely chopped shallot and salt and pepper. Once the shallot is wilted, whisk in the flour and continue to cook it over medium heat, whisking the entire time. The goal in this step is to "cook" the flour flavor out and to marry the three ingredients in the pan before adding the milk and cream. Be careful not to brown the roux; a béchamel is meant to stay white.

Second, the liquid that joins the roux—a combination of milk and cream in the basic béchamel recipe—needs to be cold when it hits the hot roux, not hot. Being on opposite ends of the temperature spectrum helps the two to come together without clumping. As the béchamel heats and begins to simmer, it will thicken to a consistency that will hold in a tilted spoon. Feel free to add more milk if you desire a thinner béchamel. Also, because it is so mild, it is important to taste and adjust the salt and pepper seasonings in a béchamel very carefully to avoid a bland sauce. After cooking for about 8 minutes, a béchamel is ready to be put to tasty good use.

SAUCE BÉCHAMEL CLASSIQUE
Basic Béchamel Master Recipe

(MAKES 3 1/2 CUPS)

This basic recipe is the starting point for myriad useful variations, as the following recipes will show.

4 tablespoons unsalted butter

1 shallot or small onion, finely chopped (about 3 tablespoons)

4 tablespoons all-purpose flour

2 cups skim milk

1 1/2 cups half & half

Sea salt or kosher salt

Ground white pepper

In a medium saucepan, melt the butter over medium heat. When just melted, add the chopped shallot or onion and whisk to combine. Continue whisking and cooking (without browning), until the shallot has softened, about 3 minutes. Whisk in the flour rapidly all at once to combine. Add the milk and half & half, drizzling rapidly into the roux, whisking continually. Season to taste with salt and pepper. Continue whisking and cooking the béchamel another 5 to 10 minutes, or until it has come to a gentle simmer and thickened to the consistency of thick chowder. Taste and adjust salt and pepper. Keep warm. Any leftovers can be stored in the refrigerator in a sealed container for up to 3 days and gently reheated for another use.

Note: To limit the fat and calories, the recipe can be prepared with skim milk only, unless it will be flavored with alcohol or acid in the recipe where it will ultimately be used. Depending on the quantity, you might risk breaking (curdling) the sauce.

MAÏS À LA CRÈME AVEC THYM FRAIS ET CRUMBLE DE BACON
Creamed Corn with Fresh Thyme and Bacon Crumbles

(MAKES 4 TO 6 SERVINGS)

Fresh, sweet seasonal corn gets all creamy and delicious with flavor mates fresh thyme and bacon. This would be grand as a sauce or a side to a grilled steak or hamburger.

2 cups Basic Béchamel (page 32)

3 cups fresh corn cut off the cob (about 5 ears)

1 tablespoon sweet vermouth

2 tablespoons chopped fresh thyme

Sea salt or kosher salt

Freshly ground black pepper

3 thick slices bacon

Place the béchamel into a medium saucepan over medium heat and stir frequently while warming. Add the corn and stir stirring until cooked through, about 5 minutes. Add the vermouth and thyme, and taste carefully while adding salt and pepper. Meanwhile, brown the bacon in a sauté pan over medium heat until crispy. Drain on paper towels. When cool, break into crumbles. Sprinkle over the corn to serve.

CHOU-FLEUR RÔTI AVEC SAUCE BÉCHAMEL AU CHEDDAR
Roasted Cauliflower with Creamy Cheddar Cheese Béchamel Sauce

(MAKES 4 SERVINGS)

The deep orange color and tangy flavor of best-quality cheddar cheese is glorious with mellow cauliflower, which gets even sweeter and richer when roasted in the oven. This sauce would pair beautifully with many vegetables, e.g., broccoli, potatoes, onions, and leeks. It would be heavenly as a makeshift fondue for dipping raw vegetables as well. Just be sure to keep it nice and warm. Wine added at the end makes this sauce sublime.

For the sauce:
2 cups Basic Béchamel (page 32)
2 cups lightly packed grated sharp Cheddar cheese
1 tablespoon butter
2 tablespoons best-quality white wine
   (e.g., Chardonnay)
Sea salt or kosher salt
Freshly ground black pepper

For the cauliflower:
1 large head cauliflower
2 tablespoons olive oil
Sea salt or kosher salt
Freshly ground black pepper
2 tablespoons freshly chopped parsley, optional

Preheat oven to 450° F.

Warm the béchamel sauce over medium heat. To finish, whisk the cheese into the warm sauce in three handfuls, until melted and smooth. Whisk in the butter until melted and incorporated. Whisk in the wine. Taste and adjust salt and pepper. Keep warm over low heat.

Rinse the cauliflower head thoroughly. Cut the base from the cauliflower head, pulling off any external leaves. Cut it into quarters, and cut away the tough solid core from each quarter. This will expose the florets, or bunches of crinkly cauliflower bites. Pull these apart into about 2-inch chunks. Toss in a roasting pan with the olive oil and a bit of salt and pepper. Roast in preheated oven, stirring two or three times, for about 25 minutes, or until tender and very lightly browned.

Serve cauliflower on individual plates or a platter with a generous portion of sauce. Garnish with fresh parsley if desired. This dish would be impeccable with roast beef or steak.

GRATIN CROUSTILLANT AUX CREVETTES ET AU CRABE
Crunchy Shrimp and Crab Gratin

(MAKES 16 TO 18 APPETIZER SERVINGS OR 6 TO 8 ENTRÉE SERVINGS)

Equally scrumptious as an appetizer served with warm toast triangles for dipping, or as a super satisfying entrée with a simple green salad, this rich gratin resonates with deep seafood flavor. For beautiful individual presentations, use small ramekins or scallop shells, and reduce cooking time by about 5 minutes.

2 cups Basic Béchamel (page 32)

1 tablespoon sweet vermouth

2 tablespoons Shellfish Fumet/Glace (page 29) or commercial seafood demi-glace (page 28)

2 scallions, trimmed and finely chopped

2 tablespoons finely chopped fresh parsley

1/2 teaspoon Old Bay Seasoning

Generous dash Tabasco Sauce

1/2 teaspoon fresh lemon juice

Sea salt or kosher salt

Freshly ground black pepper

1 pound fresh shrimp, peeled, deveined, and coarsely chopped

1/2 pound lump crabmeat

1/2 cup plain bread crumbs

3 tablespoons melted butter

Zest of 1 lemon

Preheat oven to 375° F.

Prepare or reheat the bechamel. In a medium saucepan, combine the warm béchamel with the vermouth, glace, scallions, parsley, Old Bay Seasoning, Tabasco Sauce, and lemon juice. Whisk to combine. Taste and adjust salt and pepper.

Arrange the shrimp in a single layer in a medium baking dish. Arrange the crab in an even layer on top. Pour the béchamel over the top and spread with a spatula to make it even.

Combine the bread crumbs with the butter and lemon zest and distribute evenly over the top. Bake on the center oven rack for 20 to 25 minutes, until bubbling and lightly browned. Serve warm.

Lasagne aux Champignons Sauvages, Morilles et Poireaux avec Sauce Mornay

Creamy Wild Mushroom, Morel, and Leek Lasagna with Fresh Thyme Mornay Sauce

(MAKES 8 TO 10 SERVINGS)

The addition of cheese (in this case a tangy Port Salut) to the béchamel transforms it into a silky, creamy Mornay sauce, which is simply a béchamel fortified with cheese. The addition of fresh thyme, slightly sweet Marsala wine, and the liquor from the presoaked dried morels gives the sauce an earthy layer of flavor depth that cloaks the mushrooms and pasta with extreme gooey goodness in every bite. Though it may seem a bit time-consuming, preparation really boils down to four simple parts: sautéing the vegetables, cooking the lasagna, preparing the béchamel, and assembling. It can be assembled the day before, refrigerated, and baked just prior to serving. (Note: All the mushrooms should have the very tips of their feet trimmed, and the fresh mushrooms should be brushed with a damp cloth to remove any dirt).

$1/2$ ounce dried morel mushrooms

1 cup best-quality dry Marsala wine

For the vegetable filling:

4 tablespoons olive oil

2 leeks, cleaned (page 23), trimmed, quartered, and finely sliced

6 cups finely sliced shiitake mushrooms

3 cups coarsely chopped portobello mushrooms

Sea salt or kosher salt

Ground white pepper

$1/2$ cup best-quality dry Marsala wine

3 tablespoons dry white wine (e.g., Chardonnay or Pinot Grigio)

Reserved morel mushrooms, coarsely chopped

For the pasta:

Boiling salted water

1 pound dried lasagna

3 tablespoons olive oil

For the cheese filling:

2 cups ricotta cheese

$1/2$ cup grated fresh mozzarella cheese

1 cup grated Parmesan cheese

For the Mornay sauce:

$3^1/2$ cups Basic Béchamel (page 32)

Reserved Marsala from the re-hydrated morels

2 tablespoons chopped fresh thyme

$1/2$ teaspoon ground nutmeg

$1/2$ cup coarsely chopped Port Salut cheese (or substitute Swiss or fontina cheese)

Sea salt or kosher salt

Ground white pepper

> continued

Place the dried morels and 1 cup Marsala in a medium glass bowl. Microwave on high for 1 minute. Set aside.

Meanwhile, heat the olive oil in a large, deep sauté pan over medium-high heat. Add the leeks, stirring to coat. Cook for about 5 minutes, or until softened. Add the shiitake and portobello mushrooms. Season lightly with salt and pepper. Stir to coat and continue cooking until softened, about 10–12 minutes over medium-high heat. Taste and adjust salt and pepper. Increase heat to high. Add 1/2 cup Marsala and boil to reduce to about 1 tablespoon. Repeat with the white wine. Squeeze any liquid out of the rehydrated morels, reserving the Marsala for later use in the Mornay. Chop the morels coarsely and add to the pan with the leeks and mushrooms. Heat through. Remove the sauté pan from the heat and set aside.

Bring a large pot, such as a stock pot, of cold water to a boil. Season liberally with salt (it should taste as salty as the sea). When the water is boiling, add the pasta and olive oil. Cook according to package directions for al dente doneness, usually about 8 minutes.

Measure out the ricotta, mozzarella, and Parmesan; set aside.

Prepare the béchamel. While it is still warm, whisk in the reserved Marsala from the rehydrated morels, thyme, nutmeg, and Port Salut cheese. Over medium heat, whisk in all the ingredients, continuing to whisk until all of the cheese has melted. Taste and adjust salt and pepper.

Preheat the oven to 375° F.

Oil a lasagna pan or large casserole pan lightly with olive oil, spreading a thin layer evenly with a paper towel. Have all of your assembly ingredients nearby. Begin with 1 cup of the Mornay sauce on the bottom of the pan, spreading with a spatula to make it even. Top that with a layer of 5 or 6 slightly overlapping lasagna noodles. Layer on 2 cups of the mushroom/leek mixture. Next, spread 1 cup of ricotta evenly, then top with 1/2 cup of the Parmesan. Top this with a layer of 1 cup Mornay sauce spread evenly, and another layer of lasagna noodles. Top with the remaining mushroom mixture and then the remaining ricotta. Add another cup of the Mornay sauce, spread evenly, and another layer of lasagna noodles. To finish, add the remaining Mornay sauce and spread evenly.

Cover the pan tightly with foil and bake for 25 to 30 minutes. Remove foil and add the remaining Parmesan and fresh mozzarella, scattered evenly over the top. Re-cover with the foil and bake another 10 minutes. Remove cover and bake 5 more minutes. Remove from the oven and let rest for 1 to 5 minutes. Cut into rectangular pieces and serve hot, garnished with a few fresh thyme sprigs.

ASPERGES RÔTI AVEC ORANGE, PROSCIUTTO ET SAUCE BÉCHAMEL À LA CIBOULETTES

Roasted Asparagus with Orange, Prosciutto, and Chive Béchamel Sauce

(MAKES 4 TO 6 SERVINGS)

Roasting asparagus, or really any vegetable, increases the intensity of the flavor and renders it slightly sweet. Here, the tender spears get dressed with a sprite béchamel, rife with fresh orange juice, bits of green and mild onion flavor from the chives, and salty, pale pink ribbons of prosciutto. This dish would be beautiful with a side of scrambled eggs and a fresh baguette for any occasion where "pretty" and "delicious" are on the menu. A side of poached or sautéed salmon would also pair beautifully with this dish.

1 pound fresh asparagus

2 tablespoons olive oil

Sea salt or kosher salt

Ground white pepper

2 cups Basic Béchamel (page 32)

Zest from 1 orange

1/4 cup fresh orange juice

1/4 cup chopped fresh chives

3 pieces prosciutto, cut into thin ribbons

Preheat oven to 500° F.

Trim about 1 to 2 inches off the base of the asparagus. Peel the outer skin lightly from the base of the asparagus, about 2 inches high on each spear (this adds to the eye appeal and tenderizes the flesh). Place the asparagus in a roasting pan and toss with olive oil, salt, and pepper. Roast for 20 minutes, tossing once or twice, until softened but still having a mild crunch. Remove from the oven and cover with foil to keep warm.

Meanwhile, prepare the béchamel. Stir the zest, orange juice, chives, and prosciutto into the warm sauce. Taste and adjust salt and pepper. Arrange the asparagus on a serving platter or individual plates. Dress with warm béchamel. Serve immediately. (Any leftover sauce can be passed in a sauceboat.)

GRATIN AUX AUBERGINES ET AUX TOMATES AUX ÉPINARDS RÔTIS À L'AÏL

Spinach and Roasted Garlic-Laced Eggplant and Tomato Gratin

(MAKES 8 GENEROUS SERVINGS)

A paste of mellowed roasted garlic and slivers of wilted fresh spinach run through the béchamel that binds layers of sliced fresh tomatoes and eggplant in this simple and divine gratin. A kind of noodle-free lasagna, it's hearty enough to serve as a meatless main course with a leafy salad side and a baguette for sopping up the fabulous sauce.

5 large garlic cloves, peeled

1 teaspoon plus ¼ cup extra virgin olive oil, divided

1 medium eggplant, sliced ¼ inch thick

Sea salt or kosher salt

Freshly ground black pepper

2 medium-size ripe tomatoes, sliced ¼ inch thick

10 ounces fresh spinach, coarsely chopped
   (about 7 cups)

For the béchamel:

3½ cups Basic Béchamel (page 32)

2 tablespoons finely chopped fresh oregano, plus
   optional sprigs for garnish

Zest of 1 lemon

Generous pinch of ground nutmeg

Generous pinch of paprika

Reserved chopped spinach

Sea salt or kosher salt

Ground white pepper

1 cup plain bread crumbs

Preheat oven to 450° F.

Wrap the garlic cloves in a small piece of aluminum foil and drizzle lightly with 1 teaspoon olive oil. Twist the foil closed and roast garlic in the oven until softened, about 40 minutes. Remove from oven and set aside to cool. Reduce oven temperature to 350° F. When the garlic is cool enough to handle, spread into a paste using a chef's knife. Reserve.

Meanwhile, in a large sauté pan, sauté the eggplant in batches over medium-high heat. For each batch, pour in about 1 tablespoon of the ¼ cup of olive oil. When oil is bubbling, add eggplant slices in a single layer; season lightly with salt and pepper. Turn when the first side is golden brown, after 2 to 3 minutes, and sauté the second side. Arrange the slices on a plate as they come out of the sauté pan; reserve.

Prepare the tomatoes and spinach, removing any tough stems from the spinach with a knife before chopping.

Prepare the béchamel. To finish it, whisk in the reserved garlic paste, oregano, lemon zest, nutmeg, paprika, and reserved chopped spinach. The spinach will take a few minutes to wilt down. Taste and adjust salt and pepper.

To assemble the gratin, spread 1 cup of the béchamel on the bottom of a lasagna or casserole pan (about 4 inches deep and at least 6 by 9 inches wide). Top with a layer of tomato and eggplant slices, alternating one of each in each row of the layer. Top this with a layer of 2 cups of the béchamel, and then evenly distribute $1/2$ cup bread crumbs. Repeat with another layer of tomato and eggplant slices. Top with the remaining béchamel, spread evenly across the top, and an even dusting of the remaining bread crumbs. Cover with aluminum foil and bake for 35 minutes, or until bubbling and lightly browned. Increase heat to 400° F., remove the foil, and bake for an additional 15 minutes.

Remove from oven and let rest at room temperature for 10 minutes. Slice into large rectangles and serve. Garnish with a few sprigs of fresh oregano if desired.

Œufs Brouillés avec Sauce Béchamel aux Saucisses et à la Sauge sur Baguette Grillée

Soft Scrambled Eggs Cloaked with Sage and Sausage Béchamel Sauce on Baguette Toast Points

(MAKES 4 GENEROUS SERVINGS)

Slightly decadent and ever so yummy, this flavorful, earthy dish is ultimately comforting and perfect for breakfast, lunch, dinner or brunch. Ready in just minutes, this will be an easy favorite when entertaining or feeding a hungry crowd.

12 ounces loose pork sausage

Sea salt or kosher salt

Ground white pepper

2 cups Basic Béchamel (page 32)

1 teaspoon dried, ground sage

2 tablespoons dry vermouth

2 tablespoons pork or veal demi-glace (homemade or commercial; see page 28)

For the toast points:

8 ($^1/_2$-inch-thick) diagonally cut slices fresh baguette bread

For the eggs:

8 large eggs

$^1/_4$ cup half & half

4 tablespoons unsalted butter

Sea salt or kosher salt

Ground white pepper

4 sage leaves, optional for garnish

Heat a large sauté pan or skillet over medium-high heat. Crumble the sausage into the pan and season lightly with salt and pepper. Cook, stirring occasionally, until lightly browned and cooked through, about 5 minutes. Drain the sausage in a colander, straining off and discarding all of the rendered fat. Set aside.

Prepare the béchamel. Finish by whisking in the sage, vermouth, and demi-glace. Stir in the reserved sausage. Taste and adjust salt and pepper. Keep warm over very low heat.

Toast the sliced bread in batches in a toaster or under a high broiler until golden brown. Set aside.

In a medium bowl, whisk together the eggs and half & half until very well incorporated, aerated, and lemony in color. Melt the butter in a large skillet over low heat. Pour egg mixture into the

skillet and season lightly with salt and pepper. Continue cooking over low heat, stirring constantly with a spatula or spoon. As soon as the eggs begin to set, remove from the heat.

To serve, arrange two of the toast points each on four large plates. Divide the eggs and warm béchamel over the toast points. Serve immediately. Garnish with fresh sage leaves, if desired.

SCRAMBLED PERFECTION UNSCRAMBLED

The key to tender, soft scrambled eggs is to keep the heat nice and low. High heat toughens the protein in eggs, and so does overcooking them. Take them off the heat when they still look a little soft. Remember, they will continue to cook off the heat. A small addition of milk or cream helps keep them extra soft and tender, and goes so well with this flavorful sauce.

Queue de Homard, Palourdes et Pétoncles à la Sauce Béchamel au Safran et à la Ciboulette

Lobster Tail, Littleneck Clams and Sea Scallops with a Saffron, Chive, and Butter Béchamel Sauce

(SERVES 4 GENEROUS APPETIZER PORTIONS OR MODEST ENTRÉES)

Butter, so revered in France, gives the sauce a silky round finish that is perfect with seafood, in particular lobster, clams, and scallops. In this recipe, the sauce also gets a gorgeous flavor kiss from the seafood poaching liquid, white wine, lemon, saffron, and fresh chives. Saffron, plucked from crocus stamens, gives the sauce a luscious golden red hue and a subtle, delicate flavor. (Note: Don't over-use saffron. Too much gives a medicinal taste, but just the right amount makes the sauce taste grand.)

This is an extremely elegant offering, and deceptively easy and fast to make. I love using lobster tails because it means not having to mess with whole (live) lobsters, and the presentation is very pretty. This sauce would also be lovely with fish, especially flounder or salmon.

For the sauce:

2 cups Basic Béchamel (page 32)

$^1/_4$ teaspoon (about 8) saffron threads

Plus:

Juice of 1 lemon

3 tablespoons butter

$^1/_4$ cup reserved lobster/clam poaching liquid (see below)

3 tablespoons finely chopped fresh chives

Sea salt or kosher salt

Ground white pepper

For the poached seafood:

4 (2.5-ounce) lobster tails, shells on

16 littleneck clams, well rinsed

$^1/_2$ cup good-quality dry white wine (e.g., Chardonnay or Pinot Grigio)

$^3/_4$ cup water

Pinch of sea salt or kosher salt

For the seared scallops:

2 tablespoons unsalted butter

1 tablespoon olive oil

6 large fresh sea scallops

Sea salt or kosher salt

Ground white pepper

> *continued*

Make the béchamel according to the master recipe on page 32, adding the saffron after the milk is incorporated.

While it's cooking and beginning to thicken, prep the lobster and clams by rinsing them separately and well under cold water. Bring the wine, water, and pinch of salt to a simmer in a large, deep skillet over medium-high heat. Add the lobster rounded side down to the simmering poaching liquid, and cover the pan. Poach for about 3 minutes, turn the tails over, and cook another 1 or 2 minutes, until the flesh is opaque but still tender. Remove and wrap tightly in aluminum foil to keep warm. Add the clams to the poaching liquid and cook covered until all the clams are open and tender, about 2 to 3 minutes. Remove the clams with a slotted spoon and reserve warm with the lobster tails. Strain the poaching liquid through cheesecloth to remove any grit the clams may have released. Set aside.

Return to finishing the sauce. Whisk in the lemon juice, butter, and $1/4$ cup of reserved poaching liquid. Whisk in the chives. Taste and adjust salt and pepper. Keep warm over very low heat (do not boil aggressively, especially after the butter has been added), whisking every few minutes.

For the scallops, heat the butter and oil in a large skillet (avoid nonstick in order to achieve a nice crunch and color on the scallops) over medium-high heat. Pat each scallop dry, removing and discarding the tough muscle where it was attached to the shell. Season lightly with salt and pepper. When the butter and oil are sizzling, add the scallops. Sear for 3 minutes, or until golden and crisp on the first side; turn and cook on the second side for another 2 to 3 minutes.

Remove the shell from the reserved lobster tails by cutting through the underside of the shell with kitchen scissors. Carefully pry the whole tail from the flesh. To serve, arrange a tail towards the center of a large plate, with several clams off to the side and two scallops per plate. Spoon the sauce in a generous pool at the bottom of each plate. Serve immediately.

CROQUE-MONSIEUR AU ROMARIN ET À LA MOUTARDE DE DIJON
Rosemary-Dijon Croque-Monsieurs

(MAKES 6 SANDWICHES)

De rigueur at bistros and cafés across France, a croque monsieur is a gloriously dressed-up version of a grilled ham and cheese sandwich, with the added bonus of a creamy béchamel. Here, fresh rosemary and Dijon mustard take these special sandwiches to a new level. Delicieux!

2 cups Basic Béchamel (page 32)
1 tablespoon finely chopped fresh rosemary, plus
   more for garnish, optional
3 tablespoons Dijon mustard
Sea salt or kosher salt
Ground white pepper

12 slices fresh soft white bread
18 slices best-quality thinly sliced smoked ham
1 1/2 cups grated Gruyère cheese
6 tablespoons butter, room temperature

Prepare the béchamel. When completely cooked and thickened, whisk in the rosemary and Dijon mustard. Taste and adjust salt and pepper.

To assemble each sandwich, spread about 1 tablespoon of the béchamel on the interior side of two slices of bread. Top this with 3 slices ham and about 1/4 cup of the grated Gruyère. Gently close the sandwich together, and evenly butter the exterior of each slice with about 1 teaspoon softened butter.

Cook over a medium to medium-high grill or sauté pan, gently flipping once or twice with a spatula, until the bread is golden brown on the outside and the cheese is melting, about 5 minutes total per sandwich.

Cut each sandwich in half at a diagonal and serve warm. The sandwiches can also be cut into smaller pieces and pierced with a toothpick for enticing aperitifs. Garnish with fresh rosemary if desired.

Poulet à la Crème de Champignons et aux Poireaux avec Moutarde de Dijon et Persil sur lit de Pâtes

Cream of Mushrooms, Leeks, and Chicken with Dijon Mustard and Fresh Parsley over Noodles

(MAKES 6 GENEROUS ENTRÉE PORTIONS)

This béchamel-based sauce is reminiscent of cream of mushroom soup but in a very sophisticated way. The chunky/smooth nature of the sauce makes it the perfect candidate to dress broad egg noodles. A small amount of chopped or shaved truffle would make an excellent addition to the mushroom sauce, but the Dijon and parsley work flavor wonders. The sauce can be prepared ahead and gently reheated over medium heat.

2 tablespoons unsalted butter

2 garlic cloves, finely chopped

3 leeks

Sea salt or kosher salt

Ground white pepper

8 ounces fresh button mushrooms, coarsely chopped

3 boneless, skinless chicken breasts (about 2 pounds), cut into $1/4$-inch dice

3 tablespoons Marsala wine

For the noodles:

1 pound dry, wide egg noodles

2 tablespoons freshly chopped thyme or lemon thyme, optional

For the béchamel:

$3^1/_2$ cups Basic Béchamel (page 32)

$1/_2$ cup Chicken Stock (page 24)

3 tablespoons Dijon mustard

$1/_4$ cup finely chopped fresh parsley leaves

Melt the butter in a large, deep skillet over medium heat. Add garlic and cook to soften, 1 to 2 minutes. Trim the root base and all but 1 inch of green off the leeks. Clean the leeks according to "Cleaning Leeks" page 23. Cut lengthwise into quarters. Bunch the quartered bundles together and chop finely with a chef's knife. Add to the skillet. Season lightly with salt and pepper. Add the mushrooms, stir, and cook for 5 minutes, until the mushrooms have softened. Add the chicken, stir, and continue to cook over medium heat until the chicken has cooked through, about 10 to 15 minutes, stirring occasionally. Add the Marsala and cook until reduced by half. Remove pan from the heat and set aside. Taste and adjust salt and pepper.

For the noodles, fill a large pot full of cold water and salt generously. Bring to a boil over high heat.

Meanwhile, prepare the béchamel according to the directions outlined on page 32. To finish, whisk in the chicken stock, reduced Marsala, mustard, and parsley. Keep warm on very low heat.

When the water for the noodles is boiling, add the noodles all at once, stir, and cook until al dente, about 8 minutes. Drain the noodles in a colander.

To serve, put a heap of noodles in a shallow, pretty bowl, and dress generously with the sauce. Garnish with fresh thyme or lemon thyme leaves if desired.

Côtelettes de Porc Sautées à la Sauce Soubise
Sautéed Pork Chops with a Soubise Sauce

(MAKES 2 1/4 CUPS SAUCE, ABOUT 4 SERVINGS WITH THE CHOPS)

Traditionally, a sauce soubise was prepared with puréed rice as a thickening agent. Here, it is prepared with a basic béchamel fortified with sautéed sweet onions, pork demi-glace, and dry vermouth. Snow white, frothy, and savory, it's perfect with big, juicy pork chops. However, it also would pair beautifully with steak or roasted chicken (see Roasted Chicken, page 71). If you do either of the latter, omit the pork demi-glace and substitute with a tablespoon or two of any of the pan drippings from the beef or chicken cooking process.

3 tablespoons unsalted butter

1 large sweet onion (e.g., Vidalia), finely chopped
(about 2 cups)

Sea salt or kosher salt

Ground white pepper

For the béchamel:
2 cups Basic Béchamel (page 32)

Reserved sautéed onions

Plus:

2 tablespoons pork demi-glace

Pinch of ground nutmeg

Sea salt or kosher salt

Ground white pepper

For the chops:
4 (2-inch-thick) bone-in, well-marbled pork chops

Sea salt or kosher salt

Freshly ground black pepper

2 tablespoons unsalted butter

2 tablespoons olive oil

1 tablespoon dry vermouth

In a large sauté pan, melt 3 tablespoons butter over medium heat. When bubbling, add the onion. Season lightly with salt and pepper. Stir to coat, and cook gently, stirring occasionally, until softened but not browned, about 5 minutes. Set aside.

Meanwhile, in a medium saucepan, prepare basic béchamel according to directions on page 32. Add the cooked onions to the finished basic béchamel, stir, and simmer over low heat for 15 minutes, adding a splash more milk if needed to thin. Purée the sauce in a food processor or blender until very smooth. Strain through a fine China cap or chinois. Return sauce to a clean saucepan and whisk in the demi-glace. Taste and adjust salt and pepper.

Separately season the pork chops generously on both sides with salt and pepper. Heat the butter and oil together in a large sauté pan over medium-high heat. When sizzling, add the pork chops. Cook on one side until golden brown, about 5 minutes. Flip and repeat on the second side for another 5 minutes. Remove the chops from the pan, cover with foil, and let rest for 10 minutes.

Discard all excess fat from the sauté pan. Heat the pan over high and deglaze with the vermouth, cooking down to a glaze and scraping up any brown bits. Strain through a China cap or chinois directly into the reserved Sauce Soubise.

Serve each pork chop with a generous side of sauce. Sautéed bitter greens such as kale or spinach would make a pleasing accompaniment.

CHAPTER 3

LES SAUCES VELOUTÉS
Velvety Sauce Delights

Velouté is a little like béchamel but a bit more grown up. The binding unit is, as with a béchamel, a blond roux. However, instead of milk, the second flavor base is white veal stock, chicken stock, or fish fumet (see Stocks chapter, page 19). This is then reduced, along with cream, to create another heavenly concentration of flavor. The combination of these ingredients, plus light salt and pepper seasoning, forms the essence of what I call a sauce velouté base and, as such, can be served as a simple sauce to top poultry, seafood, vegetables, and more.

From here, myriad derivatives of the sauce velouté base can be formed, depending on what it's going to be paired with on the plate and what flavors merge from the cooking process of whatever it will be paired with—for example, the reduced wine and swirl of butter in a White Wine and Chive Velouté (page 61), or borrowing from the cooking juices and pan drippings from a roasting chicken and mushrooms in the Sauce Suprême (page 64).

As in all French sauces, velouté derivations are designed to concentrate and maximize each layer of flavor in an efficient, waste-free, logical, and flavorful way. So,

while the order of the process may change, the basic velouté concept remains the same.

Velouté is always strained through a fine China cap or chinois before its derivative flavor agents are added to finish and define the sauce. Also, butter or a liaison of egg yolks and cream is often whisked in at the very end to add sheen, girth, and a velvety texture.

Because of its roux base, velouté is a fairly stable sauce and does not break easily. However, rather than take a risk, it is better to be safe than sorry and use heavy cream, especially when a relatively high level of acid, such as wine or lemon, is going to be added. Also, after the addition of butter or eggs, avoid a boil, especially an aggressive one. A gentle simmer is fine.

As with any sauce, seasoning should be done with an attentive palate. Multiple reductions in the case of a velouté not only concentrates flavor but also risks over-concentrating salt. Less is more in the early stages of the seasoning game here. I like the flavor and look of black pepper, but this white sauce is classically seasoned with white pepper to avoid unattractive black dots—*votre choix*.

Most importantly, if you treat velouté with respect and care and don't skip any steps—

especially skimming (see below)—this beautiful sauce will reward you with huge flavor rewards and exquisite beauty.

SAUCE VELOUTÉ "BASE"

Not all sauce veloutés are created exactly the same way, but essentially all veloutés begin with a white stock (usually veal or chicken) or fish fumet that is thickened with a roux. The veloutés are then finished with cream, wine, herbs, butter, or other savory ingredients.

It is helpful to have a sauce velouté base prepared ahead when you know you are going to be using a stock/roux reduction for a certain recipe (such as the Poulet Rôti au Sauce Suprême, page 64, or the Cabillaud Aux Sauce Vin Blanc Ciboulette, page 61). All of the variations in the sauce velouté base store very well refrigerated for a day or two, and this makes pulling together the final sauce very quick on the day you are cooking the sauce.

Because the base itself is reduced and the final velouté "small sauce" variation will often be reduced again with cream, you need to be exceptionally careful with seasoning. I recommend not seasonings at all until the later stages of the final sauce velouté preparation. Also, the butter and flour, when combined with the stock or the fumet, continually forms a skin over the top of the velouté base as it reduces—a process that takes about 1 hour. As with making stocks, set up a bowl of cold water alongside the stove, and skim the very top of the skin off with a shallow ladle as you go along. There will be more in the beginning and less as the process nears the end. Be sure to whisk frequently (after skimming, not before) so that none of the roux sticks or scalds at the bottom or sides of the saucepan.

The process for making all three sauce velouté base preparations is the same. (*Note:* if you are substituting commercial glace or bouillon, follow package directions to reconstitute and arrive at the correct quantity of stock. Usually the ratio is about 1 teaspoon of bouillon or glace per 1 cup of water.)

WHITE VEAL VELOUTÉ SAUCE BASE

(MAKES 2½ CUPS)

4 cups White Veal Stock (page 25)   2 tablespoons all-purpose flour
2 tablespoons unsalted butter

Bring stock up to a simmer in a medium saucepan (about 3-quart size) over medium-high heat. Separately, melt the butter in a small saucepan over medium heat. Whisk in the flour and continue whisking and cooking until the roux takes on a buttery, nutty aroma but still remains mostly white, about 3 minutes. Whisk half (about 2 cups) of the stock into the roux, whisking constantly to combine. Then pour the roux/stock mixture into the larger simmering stock pan. Whisk thoroughly to combine.

Bring up to a simmer over medium-high and then reduce to low. Cook very slowly, skimming and whisking, until the stock has reduced by about half (or to about 2½ cups). This will take 45 minutes to 1 hour.

Strain veal sauce through a chinois into a storage receptacle, discarding any solid bits. Cool the sauce to room temperature, cover, and refrigerate if not using immediately. Or reserve for the next step in the process for the sauce you are making.

WHITE CHICKEN VELOUTÉ SAUCE BASE

(MAKES 2¹/₂ CUPS)

4 cups Chicken Stock (page 24)

2 tablespoons unsalted butter

2 tablespoons all-purpose flour

Bring stock up to a simmer in a medium saucepan (about 3-quart size) over medium-high heat. Separately, melt the butter in a small saucepan over medium heat. Whisk in the flour and continue whisking and cooking until the roux takes on a buttery, nutty aroma but still remains mostly white, about 3 minutes. Whisk half (about 2 cups) of the stock into the roux, whisking constantly to combine. Then pour the roux/stock mixture into the larger simmering stock pan. Whisk thoroughly to combine.

Bring up to a simmer over medium-high and then reduce to low. Cook very slowly, skimming and whisking as described on page 54, until the stock has reduced by about half (or about 2¹/₂ cups). This will take 45 minutes to 1 hour.

Strain chicken sauce through a chinois into a storage receptacle, discarding any solid bits. Cool the sauce to room temperature, cover, and refrigerate if not using immediately. Or reserve for the next step in the process for the sauce you are making.

FISH FUMET VELOUTÉ SAUCE BASE

(MAKES 2 1/2 CUPS)

4 cups fish stock (page 26)

2 tablespoons unsalted butter

2 tablespoons all-purpose flour

Bring fumet up to a simmer in a medium saucepan (about 3-quart size) over medium-high heat. Separately, melt the butter in a small saucepan over medium heat. Whisk in the flour and continue whisking and cooking until the roux takes on a buttery, nutty aroma but still remains mostly white, about 3 minutes. Whisk half (about 2 cups) of the fumet into the roux, whisking constantly to combine. Then pour the roux/fumet mixture into the larger simmering stock pan. Whisk thoroughly to combine.

Bring up to a simmer over medium-high and then reduce to low. Cook very slowly, skimming and whisking as described on page 54, until the fumet has reduced by about half (or about 2 1/2 cups). This will take 45 minutes to 1 hour.

Strain fish sauce through a chinois into a storage receptacle, discarding any solid bits. Cool the sauce to room temperature, cover, and refrigerate if not using immediately. Or reserve for the next step in the process for the sauce you are making.

BLANQUETTE DE PORC, SAUCE CRÉMEUSE VELOUTÉ ET LÉGUMES
Pork in a Creamy Velouté Sauce with Vegetables

(SERVES 4 TO 6)

In France, this dish is prepared with veal shoulder and is thus called blanquette de veau. *Because finding veal in the United States is getting increasingly difficult and pricey, I used pork shoulder here, which has a mildly sweet, milky flavor, similar to veal. If you can find veal, go ahead and change it out, along with the pork demi-glace to a veal demi-glace. The stock in this dish comes from a long, gentle simmer of the shoulder (which tenderizes this tough cut to butter), along with several vegetable aromats. It is strained and finished with fresh vegetables, cream, lemon, and more to yield a truly distinctive and beautiful dish.*

2 pounds pork shoulder, sinew and excess fat discarded, cut into 2-inch cubes

5 cups water, or enough to just cover

1 onion, peeled, pierced with 5 whole cloves

1 bouquet garni (several sprigs fresh thyme and fresh parsley, and 2 bay leaves, tied in a tight bundle with kitchen string)

10 coriander seeds

5 black peppercorns

Pinch of sea salt or kosher salt

1 large carrot, peeled and cut into 2-inch lengths

1 large leek, white part only, cleaned (see "Cleaning Leeks," page 23), halved lengthwise and cut into 2-inch lengths

2 ribs celery, trimmed, rinsed, and cut into 2-inch lengths

2 cups frozen pearl onions

To finish the sauce:

2 tablespoons unsalted butter

2 tablespoons all-purpose flour

4–5 cups reserved, strained cooking broth from the pork/vegetable braise

2 tablespoons glace du porc (or substitute veal demi-glace, page 28)

1 cup heavy cream

1 tablespoon dry vermouth

Juice of 1 lemon

Sea salt or kosher salt

Ground white pepper

2 tablespoons coarsely chopped fresh chives

Place the pork and water together in a medium Dutch oven or stock pot. Bring to a simmer over medium-high heat. Add the whole onion with cloves, bouquet garni, coriander seeds, peppercorns, and a small pinch of salt. Once at a full simmer, reduce to low and simmer uncovered until the pork is very tender, 1 1/2 to 2 hours. Periodically skim off and discard any foam or scum that rises.

> *continued*

CREVETTES À LA SAUCE VELOUTÉ AU CURRY ET AU LAIT DE COCO
Shrimp in Curry and Coconut Milk Sauce

(SERVES 4 TO 6)

Both curry powder and coconut milk play sweetly with fresh shrimp, making a silky and luxurious dish. This velouté begins with a fish fumet base (previously prepared) that is fortified with a ready-made glace from the flavorful shrimp shells, curry, and coconut milk. Though often associated with India, curry powder—a blend of several spices—is used frequently in French classical cuisine. This recipe calls for a relatively mild yellow curry blend, but feel free to step up the heat with a red curry.

Shrimp Shell Glace
1 pound large (20–24 count) raw shrimp, shells on
1 cup water, or enough to cover shrimp shells

For the sauce:
2 tablespoons unsalted butter
1 large shallot, finely chopped
Pinch of sea salt or kosher salt
Ground white pepper

1 tablespoon plus 1 teaspoon yellow curry powder
2 1/2 cups Fish Fumet Sauce Velouté Base
  (page 57)
1 cup coconut milk
2 tablespoons reserved shrimp shell glace (above)
1 teaspoon honey, optional
Reserved shrimp
2 tablespoons chopped fresh basil leaves

Rinse the shrimp thoroughly under cool water. Peel and devein the shrimp. (*Note:* I suggest cutting through the shells on the rounded back side of each shrimp just to expose the vein. Remove the shell by unwrapping from around the body of the shrimp; save the shells separately. Remove and discard the veins. Rinse shells and shrimp well before proceeding.) Cut the shrimp into 1-inch-long chunks and reserve. Place the shells in a medium saucepan and just cover with cold water. Bring to a boil then reduce to a simmer. Continue cooking until there are 2 to 3 tablespoons of water left in the pan. Strain out the shells and discard, reserving the glace.

Meanwhile, melt the butter in a medium saucepan over medium heat. Add the shallot and cook until just softened, about 3 minutes. Season lightly with salt and pepper. Add the curry powder, stir, and cook 1 more minute. Add the previously prepared Fish Fumet Sauce Velouté Base, coconut milk, and reserved glace. Bring to a simmer over medium-high heat, whisking. Cook until it is reduced to about 1 1/2 cups. Season to taste with salt and pepper. Fold in the honey, if using, and raw shrimp, and cook until the shrimp is just opaque, about 3 minutes. Serve over steamed rice and garnish with fresh basil. *Delicieux!*

POULET RÔTI À LA SAUCE SUPRÊME ET DUXELLE ROMARIN

Roasted Chicken Thighs with Supreme Sauce & Finely Chopped Sautéed Mushrooms with Fresh Rosemary

(SERVES 4)

Sauce Suprême rules supreme in classical French sauces and is one of the top contenders in the velouté category. It begins with Chicken Sauce Velouté Base reduced with cream and finished here with roasting juices from the chicken, shallots, wine, and butter. The duxelle of mushrooms gets kissed with the earthy flavor of rosemary. The chicken roasting juices and multiple reductions ultimately yield an extremely savory, complex sauce with a sun-tanned butter color. To do it all at once involves a little bit of multi-tasking but not a huge amount of time. Save some time by preparing the velouté base a day or two ahead.

2¹/₂ cups White Chicken Sauce Velouté Base
   (page 56)
1 cup heavy cream

For the chicken:
4 chicken thighs (about 2 pounds)
Sea salt or kosher salt
Ground white pepper
1 tablespoon unsalted butter
1 tablespoon olive oil

For the mushrooms:
1 tablespoon fat from the chicken sauté

1 shallot, finely chopped
Dash of sea salt or kosher salt
Ground white pepper
2¹/₄ cups finely chopped button mushrooms
1 tablespoon finely chopped fresh rosemary leaves
¹/₄ cup good-quality Chardonnay

To finish the sauce:
3 tablespoons Chardonnay
2 tablespoons unsalted butter
Sea salt or kosher salt
Ground white pepper
Parsley or rosemary sprigs for garnish

Preheat oven to 350 F.

    Start the sauce. Combine previously prepared Chicken Sauce Velouté Base with the cream in a medium saucepan. Bring to a boil then reduce to a simmer. Frequently skim off any skin that may form and whisk. Reduce to about 1¹/₄ cups; this will take approximately 45 minutes.

    Meanwhile, season the chicken thighs on both sides with salt and pepper. In a large sauté pan, heat the butter and olive oil over medium-high heat. When sizzling, arrange the chicken skin side down. Sauté for 3 minutes, or until crispy and golden on the first side. Turn and repeat on the second side. Remove pan from the heat.

> *continued*

Arrange the chicken skin side up in a separate roasting pan. Place the pan in the preheated oven and cook until the chicken juices run clear and the chicken is cooked through, about 35 minutes.

Meanwhile, drain off all but 1 tablespoon of fat from the pan in which the chicken was sautéed. Heat the pan and the fat over medium heat, and add the shallot and a fine dash of salt and pepper. Cook, stirring, for about 3 minutes. Add the chopped mushrooms and rosemary. Cook, stirring, over medium heat until the mushrooms have softened and wilted, about 8 minutes. Deglaze with 1/4 cup Chardonnay, stirring up the bits at the bottom. Cook over medium-high heat until the wine has evaporated. Set aside.

To finish the sauce, remove the cooked chicken from the oven and wrap it in aluminum foil to keep warm. Deglaze the roasting pan on the stovetop over high heat with 3 tablespoons Chardonnay. Scrape up any browned bits with a flat-edged wooden spoon. Cook until reduced to just 1 tablespoon. Whisk this reduction into the cream and chicken sauce velouté base. Strain the sauce through a chinois and return to a small saucepan. Over medium heat, whisk in the butter until incorporated and the sauce is heated through. Taste and adjust seasonings as needed.

Reheat the reserved mushrooms over medium heat. To plate, arrange a small mound of the mushrooms off-center on each plate. Perch a piece of chicken off to the side. Spoon a generous portion of warm sauce around the edges of the plate. Garnish with a sprig or two of fresh parsley or rosemary.

BOULETTES DE VEAU ET DE PORC À LA SAUCE VELOUTÉ PIQUANTE

Veal and Pork Meatballs with Piquante Velouté Sauce

(MAKES 36 MEATBALLS, OR 6 GENEROUS SERVINGS)

Finished with the sweet crunch of cornichons, sugar, and red wine vinegar, this shallot-rich classic sauce begins with a recipe of White Veal Sauce Velouté Base. It is best prepared earlier in the day, or a day or two before finishing the dish, to keep kitchen time light on service day. This is a magnificent sauce, and the meatballs are fork-tender and juicy. They are filling enough to be served alone but would also be luscious over broad-noodle pasta such as pappardelle or egg noodles. If you have difficulty finding ground veal, substitute ground pork.

For the meatballs:

1 pound ground pork

1 pound ground veal

1 egg, beaten

2 tablespoons chopped fresh parsley

1 cup plain bread crumbs

1 shallot, finely chopped

2 tablespoons Dijon mustard

1 tablespoon herbes de Provence, or dried thyme

2 teaspoons sea salt or kosher salt

1 teaspoon ground black pepper

$1/2$ cup skim milk

2 garlic cloves, minced

1 tablespoon olive oil

For the sauce:

$2^{1}/_{2}$ cups White Veal Sauce Velouté Base
(page 55)

1 cup heavy cream

2 tablespoons butter

1 large shallot, finely chopped ($1/_3$ cup)

$1/_3$ cup red wine vinegar

1 tablespoon granulated sugar

$1/_3$ cup finely chopped cornichons

Sea salt or kosher salt

Ground white pepper

Finely chopped fresh chives for garnish

Preheat oven to 350 F.

Prepare the meatballs. In a large bowl, combine all of the meatball ingredients except the olive oil. Blend thoroughly with clean hands until well blended and uniform. Form a tiny patty and sear over medium heat to cook through. Taste and adjust seasonings in the meatball mixture if necessary. (*Note:* I have measured the salt and pepper and was pleased with the seasonings in the recipe, but you may want to modify.) Form the meatballs into uniform 2-inch balls. Using a paper

> *continued*

napkin, spread 1 tablespoon olive oil on the bottom of a large roasting pan. Arrange the meatballs in a single row in the pan, spacing evenly. Bake for 25 to 30 minutes, or until cooked through and lightly browned. Remove meatballs with a slotted spoon and reserve warm in a bowl covered with aluminum foil. Drain all excess fat from the pan. Keep pan (and its brown bits) nearby for finishing the sauce.

While the meatballs are cooking, start the sauce. Bring the veal velouté base to a simmer in a medium saucepan over medium-high heat. Whisk in the heavy cream. Continue to cook, skimming and whisking as needed, until reduced to $2^1/4$ cups, about 45 minutes. Strain through a China cap into a clean medium saucepan.

Melt the 2 tablespoons butter in the reserved roasting pan on the stovetop over medium heat. Add the shallots and cook gently until softened, about 5 minutes. Add the vinegar and sugar and cook, whisking, until reduced to just 1 tablespoon. Add this mixture to the reserved sauce. Stir in the chopped cornichons. Season to taste with salt and pepper. Heat through over medium heat.

To serve, arrange 6 meatballs per serving in shallow bowls and dress generously with the warm sauce. Garnish with fresh chives. (*Note:* Both the complete sauce and meatballs can be made a day ahead and reheated together over medium-low heat or in a moderate 350-degree F. oven, covered with foil.)

POULET RÔTI À LA SAUCE POULETTE
Roasted Chicken with Poulette Sauce

(SERVES 4 TO 6)

For this dish, start by roasting a chicken. Chicken velouté base, reduced with cream and finished with butter, shiitake mushrooms, lemon, shallots, parsley, and juices from freshly roasted chicken is just as scrumptious as it sounds. It would be magnifique *with braised vegetables such as leeks or celery, or on top of a mound of mashed potatoes. This one will have you saying "ooh la la!"*

2¹/₂ cups White Chicken Sauce Velouté Base
   (page 56)

1 cup heavy cream

Sea salt or kosher salt

Freshly ground black pepper

3 tablespoons butter

1 shallot, finely chopped (about 3 tablespoons)

2¹/₂ cups finely sliced shiitake mushrooms

Juice of 1 lemon

3 tablespoons finely chopped fresh parsley leaves

1 tablespoon strained pan juices from roasted
   chicken (page 71)

1 roasted chicken (page 71), cut into 6 pieces

Fresh lemon for garnish, optional

Parsley for garnish, optional

Pour the prepared chicken sauce velouté into a medium saucepan. Whisk in the heavy cream and a pinch of salt and pepper. Bring to a low boil over medium-high heat, and then reduce to a simmer over low heat. Skim off any foam or scum as it cooks. Cook for 20 to 25 minutes, until it is reduced by half, to about 1³/₄ cups.

Separately, melt the butter in a large sauté pan over medium heat. When bubbling, add the shallot and cook, stirring, until softened, about 3 minutes. Add the mushrooms all at once, seasoning lightly with salt and pepper and stirring. Cook until softened, about 7 minutes. Add the lemon juice and parsley, stirring to combine. Season again lightly with salt and pepper.

Just before serving, whisk 1 tablespoon of the reserved roasting juices from the chicken cooking pan into the sauce, and combine the sautéed mushroom mixture with the warm sauce. Serve the chicken on individual plates or on a platter, with the sauce alongside. Garnish with fresh lemon and parsley if desired.

POULET PARFAITEMENT RÔTI
Perfect Roasted Chicken

Roasting chicken is simple and so rewarding when done with love for the people who will sit at your table. Basting is really the key; keep giving back to the chicken what it gives to you in juices. Use a sturdy roasting pan and a roasting rack to keep the chicken off the bottom of the pan; the rack enables better browning.

1 (3 to 4-pound) chicken
Sea salt or kosher salt
Freshly ground black pepper
8 sprigs fresh thyme
1 shallot, halved
1 small carrot, peeled and cut into 3-inch lengths

1 small celery rib, trimmed and cut into 3-inch lengths
2 tablespoons unsalted butter, thinly sliced

For basting:
3/4 cup good-quality white wine (e.g., Sauvignon Blanc or Chardonnay)
3/4 cup Chicken Stock (page 24)

Preheat oven to 375 F.

Rinse the chicken and pat dry. Trim off and discard wing tips and any excess fat from near the cavity. Season the cavity generously with salt and pepper. Fill the cavity with the thyme, shallot, carrot, and celery. Loosen the skin on the chicken breast from the flesh by slipping your index fingers under the skin and gently prying it loose. Place the sliced butter under the skin of the breasts, spacing evenly.

To truss the chicken, arrange it on your work surface, back side down. Run kitchen string underneath the bottom of the spine and around the bottom of the legs. Cross the string over itself and now guide it up on both sides of the breast, along the crease where the thighs and the breast meet. Flip the chicken over, wrap the string around the wings, and pull tightly to form a knot. Trim off the excess string. Season the chicken generously all over with salt and pepper. Bake until the skin is a pale golden color and skin crust forms. Reduce heat to 350 F. Combine the wine and stock and baste the chicken, starting now, every 20 to 25 minutes, or until it's done, about 1 1/2 hours. Test for doneness by piercing chicken between the leg and breast; it is cooked when the juices run clear. Remove chicken from the pan, cover with aluminum foil, and let rest for 20 minutes.

Strain the pan juice through a chinois into a small bowl. Spoon off any visible excess fat. Use 1 tablespoon of pan juice to finish the sauce for the Poulet Rôti à la Sauce Poulette avec (page 70), or anytime you want to add bonus chicken flavor to a sauce. To carve the chicken, cut the legs away from the body, and cut each into two pieces at the joint. Carve the breasts away from the carcass and cut each horizontally into two pieces.

ŒUFS DURS À LA SAUCE AURORE
Hard Boiled Eggs with Aurore Sauce

(SERVES 6 TO 8)

Classically, a sauce aurore (aurore means "dawn") is prepared with a chicken sauce velouté base that is reduced along with tomato paste and cream. Here, a splash of red wine vinegar, tarragon, and finely chopped fresh tomato finish the sauce. The gorgeous red color and gentle tomato flavor goes beautifully with eggs but also pairs amiably with roasted chicken. Add this to your memorable brunch repertoire. Eggs thinly sliced and fanned, with a pool of the sauce alongside, make a lovely dish.

For the sauce:

2 1/2 cups White Chicken Sauce Velouté Base
  (page 56)

1/4 cup tomato paste

1 cup whole cream

Sea salt or kosher salt

Ground white pepper

1 teaspoon red wine vinegar

1 teaspoon dried tarragon leaves

2 tablespoons unsalted butter

2 tablespoons finely chopped, seeded tomatoes

Tarragon sprigs for garnish, optional

For the eggs:

12 medium eggs

1 tablespoon vinegar

Combine the prepped velouté base with the tomato paste and cream in a medium saucepan. Bring to a simmer over medium heat. Season lightly to taste with salt and pepper. Reduce to a simmer over low heat. Reduce, skimming foam and scum, by about half, or to about 1 3/4 cups.

Meanwhile, gently place the eggs in a large saucepan. Add just enough cold water to cover and add 1 tablespoon vinegar. Bring to a rolling boil, then turn off heat and allow eggs to stand in the hot water for exactly 15 minutes. Drain the water from the eggs and return them to the pan with more cold water plus 2 cups of cubed ice. Chill for 10 to 15 minutes. Peel the shells from the eggs under running water and reserve.

To finish the sauce, strain it through a China cap into a fresh saucepan. Whisk in the red wine vinegar, tarragon, and butter over medium heat. Taste and adjust seasonings as needed. Stir in the tomato.

Cut the eggs into thin slices, two eggs per plate, and create a fan on each plate. Garnish with fresh tarragon sprigs if desired.

CHAPTER 4

LES EMULSIONS FROIDES
Cold Emulsion Sauces

MAYONNAISE

For most of us, mayonnaise comes in a jar. But for the enlightened, spoiled few, real mayonnaise is whipped up on the kitchen counter with farm-fresh eggs and best-quality oil. The shiny, silky real deal is truly a snap to make and so worth the few minutes it takes to make it happen. Although technically not considered a "mother sauce," mayonnaise is the delicious, ultra-versatile backbone to many classic sauces, from *rémoulade* to *rouille*. Mayonnaise (pronounced MAAH-O-nez *en français*) is an emulsion sauce that, with a little technique, marries two foreign entities—oil and egg yolks. The trick is to get them to stick together.

Whether using a food processor, a blender, or whisk and bowl, the egg yolks, a bit of Dijon mustard (a natural emulsifier), lemon juice (or another acid), and seasonings get a little wake-up call with an initial series of pulses (about 15 to 20) or a serious series of whisks. After that, the oil is very slowly incorporated in a slow stream, almost a trickle. When the mixture starts to thicken and take on a sauce-like form (usually when about a third of the total oil has been added), you can increase the speed of adding the oil, until you have a glorious, thick mayonnaise. The only way you can break the emulsification from this point is to add too much oil, keeping in mind that each yolk can absorb roughly $2/3$ cup of oil.

If the sauce breaks, it will look like a clumpy, ugly oil slick. However, there is a fail-safe method for rescuing it: put 1 tablespoon of Dijon mustard in a clean bowl. Gradually whisk the broken mayonnaise into the mustard and proceed as if you were making a regular mayonnaise, adding the sauce very slowly and whisking constantly. This will put Humpty Dumpty back together again every time.

TIPS FOR MAKING MAYONNAISE

Here are a few things to keep in mind when preparing mayonnaise:

- **Clean bowl**—Always make sure the bowl, processor, or blender you use is spotless. Any fat or lingering food particle will reduce the likelihood of a successful emulsion. Wipe it down with a paper towel dipped in vinegar before using. Use only glass or nonreactive bowls; stainless steel will discolor the sauce.

- **Right equipment**—If using a food processor, use the plastic blade. A medium-size processor bowl (around 8 cups) works best for the Master Basic Mayonnaise Recipe. It's more difficult to create the initial emulsion with a larger processor bowl. Blenders work fine but tend to make a thicker, tougher mayonnaise. A bowl and a whisk are handy, but, of course, this method requires more muscle.

- **Pasteurized eggs**—Mayonnaise is prepared with raw eggs, which makes it perishable and potentially an agent of food-borne illnesses. To prevent getting ill, use pasteurized or very fresh AA grade eggs. If you can't find pasteurized eggs, you can pasteurize your own by placing medium-size eggs in 150° F. water for exactly 4 minutes, a little longer for bigger eggs. Rinse under cold water and store in the refrigerator until ready to use. Also, always wash your hands thoroughly with soap and warm water after breaking and handling eggs.

- **Room-temperature ingredients**—All ingredients need to be at room temperature before making the mayonnaise, so take the Dijon mustard, lemons, and eggs out of the refrigerator 30 minutes before putting it together.

- **Mild-flavored oil**—Use oils such as vegetable, canola, or peanut for mayonnaise. Strong-flavored oils such as extra virgin olive may overwhelm the gentle flavors of the sauce. The Master Basic Mayonnaise Recipe (page 78) uses a combination of both and yields a delicious mayonnaise with a hint of the fruitiness of olive oil.

- **White pepper**—Always use white pepper in a mayonnaise. Black pepper is too strong and dark for this sauce.

- **Store in refrigerator**—Store the mayonnaise in a glass screw-top jar or sealed plastic container in the refrigerator; it will keep for up to 4 days. Keep it refrigerator-cold until 10 to 20 minutes before serving.

- **Flavor additions**—Above all, have fun! Once you've mastered the mayonnaise basics—and it won't take long—you can add anything you want to it, as long as it makes sense with what you are pairing it with. For example, adding diced cucumber, dill, and maybe a little whipped cream to mayonnaise would make a perfect topping for grilled salmon. Adding fish roe to mayonnaise would be an instant hit with lobster or lobster salad. Elegant truffles folded into mayonnaise would be superb with pork, beef, or chicken. Try curry, paprika, Roquefort, herbs, wine, or lemon—the ways to dress up mayonnaise as an elegant sauce are virtually endless. It's so much more than something to spread on bread or to bind a chicken salad.

SAUCE MAYONNAISE CLASSIQUE
Master Basic Mayonnaise Recipe
(MAKES 2¹/₄ CUPS)

A very pale shade of yellow nods to the beautiful fresh egg yolks, while pure oil adds sheen and body to a simple mayonnaise. A complete absence of the faux flavors of the emulsifiers and additives found in commercial mayonnaise allows unadulterated flavor to shine through.

1 tablespoon Dijon mustard

1 whole egg

2 egg yolks

1 tablespoon fresh lemon juice

1 teaspoon sea salt or kosher salt

Generous pinch of ground white pepper

1¹/₂ cups vegetable, peanut, or canola oil

¹/₂ cup extra virgin olive oil

In a food processor with a plastic blade, pulse together the mustard, whole egg, egg yolks, lemon juice, salt, and pepper until frothy, about 20 to 25 pulses. Combine the oils in a large measuring cup with a lip for pouring. Very slowly, almost at a trickle, dribble in small amounts of oil with the processor motor still running. Continue until you've added about ³/₄ cup oil. The emulsification should begin at this point, and the sauce will change from liquid to slightly thick. Add the remaining oil in a steadier stream now, until it's gone. Voila—mayonnaise! Taste and adjust seasonings. Remove from the processor and refrigerate immediately in a sealed nonreactive plastic or glass container. It will store safely for 4 to 5 days. Use as needed.

The recipes that follow call for only half of this recipe. Make an entire batch and use the mayonnaise a couple of different ways over a few days. You'll find yourself making it over and over again—it's that fabulous.

AIOLI

(MAKES 1¹/₄ CUPS)

This garlicky gem of a sauce hails from the Provence region of France. Use it with any foods that are enhanced with the pungent bite of garlic, such as boiled eggs, potatoes, fish, crudités, or chicken. Classically, aioli is the dressing that finishes the celebrated Salade Niçoise, which is prepared with many of these same ingredients (excluding chicken). The lemony bite of fresh thyme gives this mayonnaise a little unconventional flavor kick that goes especially well with chicken.

1 cup Basic Mayonnaise (page 78)
7 garlic cloves, peeled and smashed into a paste
Zest and juice of 1 large lemon

1 teaspoon chopped fresh thyme leaves
Sea salt or kosher salt
Ground white pepper

In a medium glass bowl, whisk together the prepared mayonnaise with the remaining ingredients except salt and pepper. Taste and add seasonings as needed. Cover and refrigerate until ready to use. Allow the flavors to come together for at least 30 minutes before serving.

RÉMOULADE

(MAKES 1¹/₄ CUPS)

This zesty mayonnaise pops with the crunch and flavor of sweet gherkins, capers, and ample herbs, rendering it the perfect dipping sauce or elegant topper for fried or baked seafood, poached/grilled/baked chicken and fish, and a fresh crudité tray. Best to make it within a few hours of serving so that the fresh tarragon and chervil flavors don't bleed into the sauce.

1 cup Basic Mayonnaise (page 78)

¹/₄ cup very finely chopped sweet gherkins

1 tablespoon plus 1 teaspoon finely chopped capers

1 tablespoon Dijon mustard

Generous dash of Tabasco Sauce

3 tablespoons chopped fresh parsley leaves

1 teaspoon finely chopped fresh tarragon

1 teaspoon finely chopped fresh chervil leaves

Sea salt or kosher salt

Ground white pepper

In a medium glass bowl, whisk together the prepared mayonnaise with the remaining ingredients except the salt and pepper. Taste and adjust seasonings as needed. Cover and refrigerate until ready to use.

ROUILLE

(MAKES 1 1/4 CUPS)

The French word rouille *means "rust," and this super-pungent, slightly hot sauce is so named for its lovely rusty hue. A staple in Provence, rouille is often served atop the croutons that garnish classic Provençale fish soups and stews, such as bouillabaisse. It is also excellent with grilled or poached fish and especially mild vegetables such as bell peppers and cucumbers, which offset the sauce's gentle heat. Or just serve on croutons prepared from toasted baguette slices as a tasty aperitif.*

1 cup Basic Mayonnaise (page 78)

8 saffron threads, crumbled between fingers

3 garlic cloves, finely chopped and smashed into
  a paste with chef's knife

1/4 cup very finely chopped canned pimento

1 teaspoon fresh lemon juice

1/2 teaspoon red chili pepper flakes

Pinch of paprika

Sea salt or kosher salt

Ground white pepper

In a blender or a food processor with a metal blade, combine all of the ingredients except the salt and pepper. Process until airy and smooth, about 1 minute. Taste and adjust seasonings as needed; process just to blend in. Cover and refrigerate until ready to serve.

SAUCE TARTARE

(MAKES 1¼ CUPS)

This king of seafood sauces reigns for a reason: it is luscious! The sweetness of the gherkins, saltiness of the capers, roundness of the cream, sweet, acid splash of wine, and freshness of dill make tartare a delectable painting with seafood, especially the fried variety. It's superb for topping crab cakes, as well.

1 cup Basic Mayonnaise (page 78)

2 tablespoons finely chopped fresh dill fronds

2 tablespoons good-quality white wine
   (e.g., Chardonnay or Pinot Grigio)

1 tablespoon heavy cream

1 scallion, trimmed, halved vertically, and
   finely chopped

4 sweet gherkins, very finely chopped

1 tablespoon capers, coarsely chopped

Sea salt or kosher salt

Ground white pepper

In a medium glass bowl, combine all the ingredients except the salt and pepper. Whisk to thoroughly combine. Taste and adjust seasonings as needed. Cover and refrigerate until ready to use.

Sauce Mayonnaise aux Anchois et au Persil

Anchovy and Parsley Mayonnaise

(MAKES 1 1/4 CUPS)

Fresh parsley and a dollop of white wine vinegar exquisitely counter the richness of anchovies in this sauce. Fresh and nutty colored, with bits of green, it is enticing on bread or crackers as an aperitif and works wonderfully with any sweet, mild fish, such as salmon, cod, haddock, or even lobster and scallops.

1 cup Basic Mayonnaise (page 78)

1 tablespoon anchovy paste

2 garlic cloves, finely chopped and smashed into a paste with chef's knife

1/4 cup finely chopped fresh parsley leaves

1 teaspoon white wine vinegar

1 scallion, trimmed, halved vertically, and finely chopped

Sea salt or kosher salt

Ground white pepper

In a medium glass bowl, combine the mayonnaise with remaining ingredients except for the salt and pepper. Whisk to combine thoroughly. Taste and adjust seasonings as needed. Cover and refrigerate until ready to use.

THOUSAND ISLAND DRESSING

(MAKES 1¹/₄ CUPS)

Not far removed from a rémoulade and very similar to Russian dressing, this sauce did not originate in France but likely in the 1,000 island area between the United States and Canada. Its core ingredient, mayonnaise, is French, however. The slightly sweet flavor and rosy color partner exquisitely with seafood, pastrami (as in a Reuben sandwich), and beef. And Thousand Island also doubles as a smashing salad dressing. This one is so good you can eat it by the spoonful.

1 cup Basic Mayonnaise (page 78)

1 tablespoon tomato paste

¹/₂ teaspoon red chili pepper flakes

¹/₄ cup finely chopped canned pimento

3 tablespoons Worcestershire Sauce

Dash of Tabasco Sauce

1 small green bell pepper, finely diced
 (about ¹/₄ cup)

Pinch of paprika

Sea salt or kosher salt

Ground white pepper

In a medium glass bowl, combine all of the ingredients except the salt and pepper. Whisk well to combine. Taste and adjust seasonings as needed. Cover and refrigerate until ready to use.

Sauce Mayonnaise au Citron

Lemon Mayonnaise

(MAKES 1¼ CUPS)

This mayonnaise is full of bright citrus flavor and is lush with chicken, fish, and crudités.

1 cup Basic Mayonnaise (page 78)
Zest of 2 medium lemons, finely chopped
Juice of 2 medium lemons

3 tablespoons heavy cream
Sea salt or kosher salt
Ground white pepper

In a medium glass bowl, combine all of the ingredients except the salt and pepper. Whisk well to thoroughly combine. Taste and adjust seasonings as need. Cover and refrigerate until ready to use.

SAUCE CRÉME FOUETTÉE ET MAYONNAISE AU RAIFORT ET À LA CIBOULETTE

Whipped Cream and Mayonnaise Sauce with Horseradish and Chives

(MAKES 1¹/₂ CUPS)

As light as a cloud and smooth as silk, freshly whipped cream gets folded into mayonnaise and seasoned with plucky horseradish and delicate chives. It is gorgeous on beef rib roast, as a garnish with beef pot roast, over grilled salmon, with poultry, or even as a dipping sauce for crudités. Once you try this, it will be in your sauce repertoire for life, and it comes together in just minutes. Keep in mind that the "puff" from the cream is not permanent. Thus, fold it in and refrigerate within a few hours, at most, from serving.

1 cup Basic Mayonnaise (page 78)

1 tablespoon prepared horseradish,
  or more to taste

¹/₂ teaspoon dry mustard

2 tablespoons finely chopped chives

¹/₂ cup cold heavy cream

Sea salt or kosher salt

Ground white pepper

In a medium glass bowl, thoroughly whisk together the mayonnaise, horseradish, dry mustard, and chives. In a small chilled glass bowl, whip the cream by whisking aggressively under and over the cream to mount it into stiff peaks. Whisk one-third of the whipped cream gently into the mayonnaise mixture. Using a spatula, fold the remaining cream into the mayonnaise mixture, gently stirring until just combined. Taste and adjust seasonings. Cover and refrigerate until ready to serve.

CHAPTER 5

LES EMULSIONS AU BEURRE, SAUCE HOLLANDAISE ET SAUCES DÉRIVÉES

Hollandaise and Derivatives and Mounted Butter Sauces

Of all the mother sauces, these buttery, airy yet rich beauties are some of the most beloved. Few sauces say "special" more than Sunday-morning poached eggs, ham, and English muffins topped with a silky hollandaise, or an elegant dinner of filet mignon dressed with a pungent béarnaise.

As much as they are beloved, the sauces in this class are intimidating to many because they break (curdle) easily. The truth is, they are not difficult to make, and by adhering to a few simple guidelines, it is actually difficult to break a hollandaise, and it always tastes divine.

There are two types of emulsion sauces made with butter: **hollandaise** and derivatives and **mounted butter** (*beurre rouge, beurre blanc,* and variations). In a hollandaise, egg yolks are whipped and mounted with butter and finished with lemon. In a mounted butter sauce, acids (wine, vinegar) are reduced with shallots and other seasonings to a glace and then mounted with butter to finish the sauce.

In both cases, the trick is ensure that the base is the right temperature when the butter is added, that it stays the right temperature throughout the process, and that it does not

receive any more butter than it can take. If it gets too hot or gets too much butter, it is at risk for breaking. For preparing either kind of sauce, you'll need a whisk and a slope-sided saucepan (or *sauteuse evasee*—crucial for keeping the heat stabilized). Give it your full attention during the brief, enjoyable preparation. Let's look at the details of each type of sauce separately.

HOLLANDAISE (AND DERIVATIVES)

The recipes that follow each begin with three egg yolks, which, when properly prepared, can hold up to $1/2$ pound (2 sticks, or 1 cup) unsalted butter. There is much debate about whether to use melted butter or clarified butter, but I like using cool, whole butter because I think the flavor is better. Additionally, incorporating the cool butter into the warm eggs helps regulate the temperature in the safe zone.

I also use pasteurized eggs or pasteurize them myself at home (see pasteurized eggs, page 76) for safety's sake, but if you can't find them, use the freshest AA grade eggs available.

I recommend bringing the eggs to room temperature, or close to it, before starting.

Take the butter from the freezer or fridge 30 minutes before starting. Cut it into 1/4-inch cubes, as these smaller cubes are easier to incorporate, and add them in batches of eight.

The first step is to prepare the eggs for receiving the butter:

In a saucepan over medium-low heat, whisk the eggs together vigorously. After about 3 minutes, they should start to thicken and become lemony in color, pulling away from the bottom of the pan.

Take the pan off the heat, and whisk in 2 tablespoons of the butter until it's melted and incorporated into the eggs. Return pan to stove.

Add the lemon juice and a pinch of salt at this point, both of which help stabilize the sauce.

From here, keep incorporating the remaining butter in 2-tablespoon increments, whisking a little less fervently from this point as you go.

The most crucial thing in making hollandaise is to monitor the heat. The sides of the pan should not be hot, and neither should the sauce. Both should feel just slightly warmer than the inside of your wrist, or slightly above body temperature—that is the gauge to use. Touch the sauce with a clean index finger as you go along to be sure. And, of course, it should not boil. It may take some getting used to, but practice removing the pan from the heat if things start getting too hot, whisk in butter to cool things down.

The finished product should be airy, light, and pale yellow. Season to taste and incorporate various other flavor ingredients as suggested on the facing page or in recipes that follow, and serve!

Troubleshooting: If the sauce breaks, it will look like a clumpy, ugly oil slick, but it is surprisingly easy to fix. Put 1 tablespoon Dijon mustard in a clean glass bowl. Very slowly dribble the broken sauce into the mustard, whisking. It should quickly start to emulsify. Keep drizzling the broken sauce into the bowl, more quickly now, until it's all gone. Return the sauce to a clean saucepan, heat through, and serve.

MOUNTED BUTTER SAUCES

These are a little less finicky because there are no egg yolks involved. But they deserve the same temperature respect as hollandaise and have the same guidelines in terms of how much butter the base can hold. In this case, the base is a reduction of wine, vinegar, shallots, and other flavoring agents—all reduced down to a few tablespoons. The hot reduction should rest a few minutes to cool down. Adding a tablespoon of cream at this point helps stabilize the sauce. Then add the butter in small increments, exactly as you would for a hollandaise. Often, mounted butter sauces are finished with fresh herbs, spices, and more.

Troubleshooting: However, unlike hollandaise, once a mounted butter sauce breaks, there is really no way to fix it. If you find yourself with a gloppy, broken sauce, don't throw it out. The flavored butter will be delicious whisked into other sauces such as reductions (see chapter 6, pages 105–115).

A FEW OTHER THINGS TO KEEP IN MIND

Holding warm sauces: Hollandaise and mounted butter sauces need to be held warm, not hot. It is best to make them just before service and keep them warm over another saucepan filled with warm water, whisking occasionally. Better yet, pour the sauce into a thermos and close the top. The sauces will safely hold 2 hours without breaking. Heat gently over low heat if necessary just before service. This method is virtually fail-safe.

Serving: Warm emulsion sauces should never be served over another very hot food, as this could make them break on the plate. Serve alongside, not on top of, hot grilled meats or any other hot food.

The respect you give to hollandaise will pay huge dividends in your kitchen. Once mastered, you'll find yourself returning to hollandaise and its otherworldly derivatives again and again. There are a multitude of variations on this classic sauce to play with, but I recommend you start with the classic derivatives that follow.

HOLLANDAISE VARIATIONS

By folding a couple of tablespoons of fresh orange juice into a finished hollandaise, you create a sauce Maltaise, which pairs spectacularly with roasted asparagus (see recipe for preparation in the béchamel chapter, page 31).

Or fold in 1/4 cup of whipped cream to create a fluffy, soufflé-like mousseline to pair with poached salmon.

A few tablespoons of diced peeled cucumber would add a pleasant crunch to the same sauce.

Other excellent hollandaise flavor enhancers include:

· saffron
· anchovies
· paprika
· curry
· sherry
· fresh herbs, virtually any kind

Taste and decide what flavors makes sense with the dish you are cooking.

CROQUETTES DE CRABE
Crispy Crab Cakes

(SERVES 4 TO 6)

Prepare the sauce while these yummy, easy crab cakes are sautéing, and both will be ready at the same time. They're delightful garnished with fresh chives.

2 tablespoons mayonnaise

2 tablespoons Dijon mustard

Dash of hot sauce

1 tablespoon capers, lightly chopped

1 egg yolk

1/4 teaspoon sea salt or kosher salt

Generous dash of freshly ground black pepper

1 pound lump crabmeat

1/2 cup plain bread crumbs

2 tablespoons unsalted butter

1 tablespoon olive oil

Fresh chives, optional

In a medium bowl, whisk together the mayonnaise, mustard, hot sauce, capers, egg yolk, salt, and pepper. Gently crumble the crabmeat into the mixture, discarding any errant bits of shell. Add the bread crumbs. Using clean fingers, gently combine the crab and crumbs with the mixture, being careful not to break up or shred the crab. Form 4 to 6 uniformly sized patties by gently pressing in your palms. Arrange on a plate and refrigerate for 30 minutes to set.

Heat a large sauté pan over medium-high heat. Add the butter and olive oil. Meanwhile, season the crab cakes lightly on both sides with salt and pepper. Arrange the crab cakes in a single layer in the pan, spacing evenly. Cook for 3 minutes, or until golden on one side; turn and cook on the second side for 3 minutes. Serve warm with hollandaise on the side.

SAUCE HOLLANDAISE

(YIELDS 1¹/₂ CUPS)

This mild, slightly lemony sauce is exquisite with many things, including the celebrated eggs Benedict, seafood, shellfish, poultry, and raw or roasted vegetables. Try it with the Croquettes de Crabe (page 95), and remember to serve the sauce on the side.

3 egg yolks, room temperature
14 tablespoons cool, unsalted butter cut into
  ¹/₄-inch cubes, divided

1 tablespoon fresh lemon juice
Sea salt or kosher salt
Ground white pepper

Whisk the eggs together vigorously in a slop-sided saucepan over low heat until it starts to thicken, about 3 minutes. You will begin to see the eggs leaving space at the bottom of the pan as they start to cook. Remove from the heat and whisk in 2 tablespoons of the butter until melted. Whisk in the lemon juice and a pinch of salt. Return to the heat, and whisk in and melt the remaining butter in 2-tablespoon increments. Continue until the butter is gone. Season to taste with salt and pepper.

PORT SAUCE AU VIN
Port Wine Sauce

(YIELDS 1¹/₂ CUPS)

The sweetness of the port combined with the richness of the brown veal stock in this reduction renders it the perfect companion for roasted pork.

1 small shallot, finely chopped (about ¹/₄ cup)
¹/₂ cup Brown Veal Stock (page 23) or
   commercial (page 28)
¹/₃ cup port wine
2 tablespoons whole cream

1¹/₂ cups hollandaise sauce (page 96)
Sea salt or kosher salt
Ground white pepper
1 tablespoon unsalted butter

Bring the shallot, veal stock, wine, and cream to a simmer over medium-high heat in a small saucepan. Reduce to 2 tablespoons of total liquid; this will take about 10 minutes. Cool slightly. Strain and whisk into one recipe of prepared hollandaise. Whisk in the butter at the end for added sheen and flavor.

As in the preceding recipe, it's best to prepare the reduction and the hollandaise at the same time and bring them together at the very end, when they're both still warm and at the right temperature.

BEURRE BLANC
White Wine Butter Sauce

(YIELDS 1¹/₄ CUPS)

Delicate and versatile, this buttery taste of goodness unites fabulously with chicken, shellfish, and cooked vegetables, especially asparagus and green beans. It is so scrumptious that you'll be tempted to eat it by the spoonful. It would also be an excellent companion to Croquettes de Crabe (page 95).

1 small shallot, finely chopped (about ¹/₄ cup)
¹/₂ cup good-quality white wine (e.g., Chardonnay)
3 tablespoons white wine vinegar
2 tablespoons heavy cream, divided

14 tablespoons cool unsalted butter, cut into
    ¹/₄-inch cubes, divided
Sea salt or kosher salt
Ground white pepper

In a slope-sided saucepan, combine the shallot, wine, and vinegar. Over medium-high heat, reduce to 3 tablespoons liquid, about 4 minutes. Remove pan from the heat. Whisk in 1 tablespoon cream. Incorporate 2 tablespoons of the cubed butter, whisking rapidly to melt and combine. Once airy, return the pan over low heat and incorporate the remaining butter, whisking in 2 tablespoons at a time until butter is gone. Whisk in remaining cream and adjust seasonings as needed.

Variation: For a fresh herb sauce, add several tablespoons chopped fresh thyme, parsley, or chives or a combination.

BEURRE ROUGE
Red Wine Butter Sauce

(YIELDS 1 1/4 CUPS)

Fortified with flavorful additions, this ultra-versatile sauce is a winner with salmon, monkfish, beef, and lobster—anything round and slightly sweet in flavor. Its rosy pink color is luscious to the eyes, as well.

1 shallot, finely chopped (about 1/4 cup)

1/2 cup good-quality red wine (e.g., Cabernet or Pinot)

3 tablespoons red wine vinegar

1 teaspoon whole black peppercorns

2 tablespoons heavy cream, divided

16 tablespoons (2 sticks) cool, unsalted butter cut into 1/4-inch cubes, divided

1 tablespoon chopped fresh tarragon leaves

1/3 cup finely chopped fresh parsley

Sea salt or kosher salt

Ground white pepper

In a slope-sided saucepan, combine the shallot, wine, vinegar, and peppercorns. Simmer vigorously over medium-high heat until reduced to just 3 tablespoons of liquid. Remove from the heat. Whisk in 1 tablespoon of cream. Incorporate 2 tablespoons of the butter off the heat, whisking until frothy and melted. Return the pan to the stove over low heat. Incorporate the remaining butter, whisking 2 tablespoons at a time, until the butter is gone and the sauce is light and airy. Whisk in remaining cream, tarragon, and parsley. Taste and adjust seasonings as needed.

SAUCE BÉARNAISE
A Hollandaise Finished with a Reduction of White Wine and Tarragon

(YIELDS 1¹/₂ CUPS)

Béarnaise is outstanding with beef, particularly a dressy filet mignon or a rich steak cut such as rib-eye or New York strip. The reduced white wine and the zesty finishing touch of fresh tarragon give this pale yellow sauce flavor panache that truly stands up to beef and even roasted chicken (page 71). (Note: It is probably easiest to make the reduction that follows as you prepare the hollandaise. Merge the two together at the end.)

1 small shallot, finely chopped (about ¹/₄ cup)

¹/₂ cup good-quality white wine (e.g., Chardonnay)

1¹/₂ cups hollandaise sauce (page 96)

1 tablespoon chopped fresh tarragon leaves

Sea salt or kosher salt

Ground white pepper

In a small saucepan, combine the shallot and wine; simmer vigorously over medium-high heat until reduced to 2 tablespoons. Strain, and slowly incorporate the remaining liquid into one recipe of prepared hollandaise. Whisk in tarragon to finish. Taste and adjust seasonings as needed.

CHAPTER 6

LES SAUCES PRÉPARÉES AVEC DES FONDS ET LES SAUCES REDUITS
Sauces Prepared with Stocks and Reduction Sauces

In this chapter we put the stocks and fumet created in chapter 1 (pages 19–29) to use in all kinds of wonderful ways. There are countless combinations of flavors and ingredients to work with, but the way most of these layered reduction sauces come together is very similar. The first layer is typically composed of shallots and wine or vinegar simmered together and reduced to a few tablespoons. Next, a stock or fumet is added and reduced, often with meat, vegetables, or herbs. The solids are usually but not always strained (see Sauce Lyonnaise, page 110), and the sauce is finished with a fortified wine and a bit of butter or cream for sheen and mouthfeel.

That is the most basic formula, but there are myriad derivatives. Although professional kitchens today decreasingly rely on flour and butter (either as cooked roux or in a raw *beurre manié*) as thickening agents, these ingredients are very handy in stretching out sauce quantities and kitchen budgets in home kitchens. The trick, when flour is involved, is to make sure the flour flavor is cooked out before the sauce is finished, as outlined in the recipes that follow. Also, whenever a roux is added early in the process, prior to the reduction of the stock or fumet, the sauce will always need to be skimmed as the flour proteins rise to the top.

Some of the most ancient and exquisite of classic French sauces originally were built from the browned bits or cooking juices from roasted, sautéed, or poached meats and fish. Later, chefs realized that by making stocks ahead of time, they would have concentrated flavor bases already available, so the sauces could be made independent of the cooked meats. So it is in your kitchen. However, whenever you have an opportunity to "steal" flavor from the meat or fish you will serve these sauces with—do it! For example, if you're roasting a rabbit to go with a Sauce Chasseur (page 109), deglaze the roasting pan with a bit of wine, reduce it off, and add it to your sauce. Never waste flavor in the kitchen if you can avoid it.

Keep in mind that because this sauce category makes use of several reductions to maximize flavor, using the best-quality wine, vinegar, and stocks is essential. It is helpful to have a good fortified wine collection and fresh herb garden, too. There really is no limit to what you can create on your own using your palate and creativity as guides. The recipes and techniques in this chapter will get you off to a wonderfully successful start.

SAUCE DIABLE

(YIELDS 1¹/₂ CUPS)

The fiery heat of cayenne, or in this case red chili pepper flakes, is a reflection of the name of this sauce, translated as "devil sauce." The peppery pluck lends well to grilled chicken, with which it is commonly served, but it also works wonderfully with grilled pork chops or even steak. A beurre manié—a simple raw paste of equal parts soft butter and flour—is added near the end to ensure proper thickening of the sauce without lumps. Be sure to cook the sauce for an additional 10 minutes after adding the thickener to cook out the flour taste. A very stable sauce, it can be made a day ahead and reheated over low heat. (Photo on page 104.)

2 large shallots, finely chopped (about ¹/₄ cup)

1 cup good-quality dry white wine (e.g., Chardonnay or Pinot Blanc)

3 tablespoons white wine vinegar

3 cups brown beef or veal stock (page 23)

1 teaspoon red chili pepper flakes

1 tablespoon flour

1 tablespoon unsalted butter, room temperature

1 tablespoon heavy cream

Pinch of sugar, optional

1 tablespoon chopped chives

Sea salt or kosher salt

Freshly ground black pepper

In a medium saucepan, combine the shallots, wine, and vinegar. Reduce over medium-high heat until there are just 4 tablespoons of liquid remaining, about 5 minutes. Add the stock and pepper flakes. Reduce the heat to medium and vigorously simmer for 15 to 20 minutes, until the mixture is reduced by about half, to 1¹/₂ cups. Combine the flour and butter together on a work surface, using your hands to form a paste, or *beurre manié*. Break the ball of paste into four parts, and whisk them into the sauce one by one until incorporated. Continue to cook the sauce, whisking over medium heat for another 10 minutes. Finish by whisking in the cream, sugar (if needed to counteract the heat of the pepper), and fresh chives. Taste and adjust seasonings as needed. Serve hot.

SAUCE ESPAGNOLE

(YIELDS 1¹/₂ CUPS)

This rich, beefy, slightly sweet sauce is a greatly simplified version of Escoffier's classic interpretation, which takes more time than most of us have. The "Spanish" part of the equation (i.e., espagnole) comes from the sherry added near the end of the cooking process. Serve it over noodles or with beef, pork, or chicken.

3 tablespoons butter

1 large carrot, coarsely chopped

1 stalk celery, coarsely chopped

2 onions, coarsely chopped

¹/₄ cup flour

5 cups beef stock (page 22)

2 garlic cloves, crushed

1 bouquet garni (several sprigs fresh thyme, fresh parsley, and 2 bay leaves)

¹/₂ cup tomato paste

¹/₃ cup dry sherry (or substitute Madeira)

Sea salt or kosher salt

Freshly ground black pepper

Melt the butter in a large saucepan over medium heat. Add carrot, celery, and onions and sauté until softened, but not brown, about 5 minutes. Add the flour and reduce the heat to medium low. Stir in the flour and continue cooking until the vegetables and flour are nicely browned. Add the stock, garlic, bouquet garni, and tomato paste. Simmer for 1 hour, skimming, or until the sauce is reduced by half. Strain through a chinois. (*Note:* You can make the sauce base a few days ahead and refrigerate before finishing.)

To finish, reduce the sauce by another third, or to about 1¹/₂ cups total, in a medium saucepan over medium/medium-high heat. Add the sherry and cook through another 10 minutes. Taste and adjust seasonsings.

SAUCE CHASSEUR

(YIELDS 2 1/2 CUPS)

Translated as "hunter's" sauce, chasseur *is so named because this sturdy sauce goes well with game of all sorts, including venison, rabbit, pheasant, quail, boar, and even chicken. It's also congenial with pasta. It's a simple demi-glace base, whose flavor is intensified and layered with the addition of mushrooms, shallots, Cognac, wine, and fresh herbs. Adding tomato paste is optional, but I like the flavor and slightly acidic undertone it contributes. This sauce can be made a day or two ahead, refrigerated, and reheated over low before serving.*

3 tablespoons unsalted butter

3 cups sliced cremini mushrooms (or substitute button or shiitake), feet trimmed

Pinch of sea salt or kosher salt

Freshly ground black pepper

2 large shallots, finely chopped (about 1/4 cup)

2 tablespoons Cognac

1/2 cup good-quality dry white wine (e.g., Chardonnay or Pinot Grigio)

1 tablespoon tomato paste, optional

1/4 cup beef or veal demi-glace (page 28)

1/2 cup warm water

1 tablespoon fresh tarragon leaves, lightly chopped

1 tablespoon fresh chervil, lightly chopped

3 tablespoons butter

Melt the butter in a medium saucepan over medium heat. Add the mushrooms, season lightly with salt and pepper, and stir to coat. Continue cooking over medium or medium-high heat, stirring from time to time, until all of the mushroom juices have evaporated and the mushrooms have started to lightly brown, about 10 minutes. Stir in the shallots and cook until softened, about 5 minutes. Add the Cognac and wine. Increase heat to medium-high and reduce by half, or until there is just about 1/4 cup liquid remaining. Whisk in the tomato paste if using.

Combine the demi-glace with warm water in a separate bowl and whisk to combine. Add it to the sauce. Continue to cook the sauce over medium heat for 10 minutes. Add the tarragon and chervil. Whisk in the butter one tablespoon at a time, and incorporate until melted and blended. Taste and adjust seasonings as needed. Serve hot. (*Note:* If preparing the sauce ahead, add the fresh herbs just before preparing to serve).

SAUCE LYONNAISE

(YIELDS 1¹/₂ CUPS)

Lyon, along with Paris and Strasbourg, is considered one of France's culinary kingpin cities. Onions, charcuterie, and vinegar figure prominently in Lyonnaise cuisine. This rich brown stock-based reduction sauce is infused with the flavor of onion, thyme, and wine and is extremely versatile. Try it with veal or pork chops, roasted chicken or beef, or over scrambled eggs or a simple cheese omelet. It can be prepared 1 or 2 days ahead and reheated over low heat before serving.

3 tablespoons unsalted butter

2 large onions, finely chopped (about 3 cups)

Pinch of sea salt or kosher salt

Freshly ground black pepper

³/₄ cup good-quality dry white wine (e.g., Chardonnay or Pinot Grigio)

2 cups brown beef or veal stock (page 23)

12 fresh thyme stems bound into a bundle with kitchen string

1 tablespoon butter

3 tablespoons chopped fresh parsley

Melt the butter in a medium saucepan over medium heat. Add the onions and stir to coat. Season lightly with salt and pepper. Cook, stirring every few minutes, until softened and golden brown on the edges, about 10 to 15 minutes. Deglaze with the wine, increase heat to medium-high, and reduce the wine until it amounts to ¹/₃ cup, about 5 minutes. Add the stock and the thyme bundle to the sauce. Bring to a boil over high heat, and then reduce heat to medium-low and simmer until the onions are very soft and the sauce is reduced to 1¹/₂ cups. Remove thyme bundle. Whisk in the butter until completely incorporated. Add the parsley. Taste carefully and adjusting seasonings as needed.

SAUCE POIVRADE
Classic Pepper Sauce

(YIELDS 2 CUPS)

A deep burgundy color from red wine and a final black peppercorn flavor punch at the end render this a sturdy, earthy sauce that is another winner with all kinds of game—especially pheasant—and even beef. It is slightly more time-intensive than some of the other sauces in this chapter, because the beef stock base simmers for some time with vegetable aromats and bacon for added flavor. Because the base contains flour, it will be necessary to skim it off as it rises to the surface during the cooking process (see skimming, page 54). Make the sauce ahead if desired, refrigerate 1 to 2 days, and reheat over low heat before serving.

2 slices bacon, diced

2–3 tablespoon unsalted butter, divided

2 medium onions, chopped

2 medium carrots, peeled and chopped

1 leek, cleaned (page 23) and thinly sliced

1 large shallot, sliced into thin rounds

Pinch of sea salt or kosher salt

Freshly ground black pepper

2 tablespoons red wine vinegar

2 tablespoons flour

2 cups good-quality red wine (e.g., Cabernet Savignon or Merlot)

2 cups brown veal (page 23) or beef stock (page 22)

1 bouquet garni (2 green leek leaves about 3 inches long, filled with a few sprigs thyme, parsley, and a bay leaf and wrapped with kitchen string)

2 garlic cloves, peeled and smashed

1 tablespoon crushed whole black peppercorns

1/4 cup brandy or Cognac

Heat a large saucepan over medium heat and cook the bacon, stirring occasionally, until the fat starts to render and the bacon edges become golden, about 3 minutes Add 1 tablespoon butter with the onions, carrots, leek, and shallot. Season lightly with salt and pepper, and stir to coat. Cook, stirring occasionally, over medium heat until softened and slightly browned, about 15 minutes. Stir in the vinegar and cook 1 minute, until evaporated. Sprinkle the flour over the mixture and stir to coat, cooking 1 minute. Add the wine, stock, bouquet garni, and garlic. Cook for about 1 hour, or until the liquid is reduced by half, to about 2 cups, skimming as you go. Add the crushed peppercorns and simmer another 10 minutes.

Strain the sauce through a China cap, discarding the solids. Return the sauce to a fresh pan and stir in the brandy or Cognac. Cook 5 more minutes. Taste and adjust seasonings as necessary. Whisk in 1 to 2 tablespoons butter, one at a time, to finish. Serve hot.

SAUCE MEURETTE
Deep-Red Wine and Vegetable Sauce

(YIELDS ¹/₂ CUP)

This versatile sauce comes together in about 30 minutes and is superb paired with poached eggs, fish, beef, veal, pork, and some types of game. It hails from the Burgundy region of France, so a nice, drinkable wine from the region will enhance the sauce.

1 slice bacon, diced

3 tablespoons unsalted butter, divided

1 onion, chopped

1 carrot, peeled and chopped

1 leek, cleaned (page 23) and chopped

Pinch of sea salt or kosher salt

Freshly ground black pepper

2 tablespoons beef or veal demi-glace

3 cups good-quality red wine (e.g., Burgundy)

1 bouquet garni (2 green leek leaves about 3 inches long, filled with a few sprigs thyme, parsley, and a bay leaf and wrapped with kitchen string)

1 tablespoon red wine vinegar

Heat a medium saucepan over medium heat and cook the bacon for 5 minutes, stirring occasionally, until the fat starts to render and the edges turn a light golden color. Add 1 tablespoon butter, onion, carrot, leek, and a pinch of salt and pepper. Stir to coat and cook for 15 minutes, or until the vegetables are softened and very lightly browned. Stir in the demi-glace and cook through, about 1 minute. Add the red wine and bouquet garni. Bring to a boil and then reduce to a simmer, skimming off any fat along the way; cook for 30 minutes. Strain sauce through a China cap into a smaller clean saucepan; discard solids. Reduce to ¹/₂ cup over medium heat. Off the heat, whisk in 2 tablespoons butter, one at a time, and the vinegar. Taste and adjust seasonings as needed. Serve hot.

SAUCE BORDELAISE

(YIELDS 1¹/₂ CUPS)

A bona fide special occasion sauce, this rich, unctuous beauty finishes with a petite dice of poached beef bone marrow. Ask your butcher for sliced beef marrowbones. It makes all the difference in the world in terms of flavor and texture. Serve this with roast beef or steak. It's best to make it "to order" lest the marrow break up in the re-heating process, but it will work fine if stirring is done with care, over low heat.

2 large shallots, finely chopped (about ¹/₄ cup)

²/₃ cup good-quality red wine (e.g., Bordeaux or Burgundy)

3 tablespoons unsalted butter, divided

1 tablespoon flour

3 cups warm brown beef stock

12–14 fresh thyme sprigs bundled with kitchen string

1 beef marrowbone

1 teaspoon fresh lemon juice

2 tablespoons chopped fresh parsley

Sea salt or kosher salt

Freshly ground black pepper

2 tablespoons diced bone marrow from reserved poached bone

Combine the shallots and red wine in a medium saucepan, and reduce over medium-high heat until just 3 tablespoons of the wine remain, 3 to 5 minutes. Reduce heat to medium. Whisk in 1 tablespoon butter and melt. Add flour, whisking, and cook through for 1 minute. Whisk in warm stock and thyme bundle. Bring to a high simmer over medium-high heat, then reduce to a simmer over medium-low heat.

Add the beef marrow bone. Cook, skimming along the way to remove any solids or scum that float to the top, for 20 to 30 minutes. Remove the marrow bone 8 minutes into the cooking and reserve it, warm. Once reduced to about 1¹/₂ cups, strain the sauce through a China cap, discarding the solids, and then return it to a clean saucepan over medium heat. Add 2 tablespoons butter one at a time, whisking fervently to incorporate. Add lemon juice and parsley. Taste and adjust seasonings as needed. Extract the marrow from the reserved bone, chop it into ¹/₄-inch dice, and add to the sauce just before serving.

Sauce Crémeuse au Poisson avec Safran, Citron et Basilic
Creamy Fish Sauce with Saffron, Lemon, and Basil

(YIELDS 1¹/₂ CUPS)

Though not an Escoffier classic sauce in name, reducing fish stock and cream together is a very traditional French sauce preparation method. Saffron and lemon zest simmering throughout the reduction process provides glorious color and flavor. Basil and a bit of butter at the end balance it all beautifully, making this silky sauce a winning bet to pair with any shellfish or fish. Whisk in a few tablespoons of any poaching liquid for the fish that's going alongside for added flavor.

3 tablespoons unsalted butter, divided

2 large shallots, finely chopped (about ¹/₄ cup)

Pinch of sea salt or kosher salt

Ground white pepper

²/₃ cup good-quality dry white wine
   (e.g., Sauvignon Blanc)

2 cups fish stock (page 26)

2 cups heavy cream

¹/₂ teaspoon saffron threads

Zest of 1 lemon

1 teaspoon fresh lemon juice

2 tablespoons coarsely chopped fresh basil leaves

Melt 1 tablespoon butter in a medium saucepan over medium heat. Add the shallots and a pinch of salt and pepper. Cook, stirring from time to time, for 3 to 5 minutes, or until softened. Add the wine, increase heat to medium-high, and reduce until just 3 tablespoons of the wine remain. Add fish fumet, cream (don't substitute a lighter cream or the acid from the wine may break the sauce), saffron, and lemon zest. Bring to a high simmer over medium-high heat, and then reduce heat to medium-low. Cook for 40 to 45 minutes, or until reduced by half, to 1¹/₂ cups. Strain through a chinois into a clean saucepan. Whisk in lemon juice and 2 tablespoons butter, one at a time, over low heat. Add the basil just before serving so it doesn't discolor. Taste and adjust seasonings as needed. Serve warm.

CHAPTER 7

LES SAUCES TOMATES
Tomato Sauces

Though frequently associated with Italian cuisine, tomato sauces play a significant role in French sauce making and cooking as well. One of the five mother sauces of French classical cooking, a tomato sauce can serve as a garnish to fish or meat or be tossed with pasta. The juicy meatiness of tomatoes makes them the perfect conduit for a quick, fresh, naturally thickened sauce, often enhanced with wine, garlic, onion, and fresh herbs.

When in season, fresh tomatoes are preferable to canned. Select firm, fragrant tomatoes. Plum varieties are considered ideal, but myriad heirloom varieties have magnificent flavor and color. When using canned, look for the whole peeled tomatoes, preferably San Marzano Italian imports.

Tomatoes are often peeled and seeded prior to cooking, or the seeds and skins are strained after cooking. Peeling and seeding fresh tomatoes is simple enough. Trim the stem base out of the tomatoes with a paring knife and cut a little X into the top of them. Place them in simmering hot water for about 30 seconds, or until little loose skin flaps forms around the X. Remove tomatoes from the water and submerge them in ice-cold water for several seconds. The skin will literally peel right off a ripe tomato. To seed tomatoes, cut them in half horizontally. Gently, using your fingertips, prod the seeds from the little seed pockets distributed throughout the tomatoes and discard. Don't fret if you miss a few.

One of the many advantages of tomato sauces is that they freeze beautifully for up to three months. Make a few big batches at the end of summer, when tomatoes are at their peak, and freeze in quantities you will use as fall and winter approach. Thaw, reheat, and voila!—an instant taste of summer on your plate, even when winter winds howl.

SAUCE TOMATE
Tomato Sauce with Herbs

(YIELD: 6 CUPS)

This lovely, light sauce is worth making over and over again. It simply sings with tomato flavor that dresses grilled fish or roasted chicken just as well as a bowl of spaghetti. There are countless variations on the theme, as well. Ground beef, turkey, pork, sausage, or bacon can be added in the early sauté process, or the sauce can be finished with other vegetables, including sliced mushrooms, bell peppers, and fennel. Add the fresh basil at the very end, just before serving, to maximize flavor.

3 tablespoons extra virgin olive oil

1 large onion, finely chopped (about 2 cups)

1 medium carrot, peeled and finely chopped (about $1/4$ cup)

4 garlic cloves, peeled, mashed, and finely chopped

Pinch of sea salt or kosher salt

Freshly ground black pepper

6 medium tomatoes, peeled, seeded, and coarsely chopped

$1/2$ cup good-quality red wine

$1^1/2$ cups chicken stock (page 24)

4 sprigs each fresh rosemary, thyme, and oregano, tied in a bundle with kitchen string

1 teaspoon sugar

Pinch of red chili pepper flakes

$1/4$ cup coarsely chopped fresh basil leaves

In a large pot or Dutch oven, heat the olive oil over medium heat. Add the onion, carrot, garlic, and a pinch of salt and pepper. Stir to coat, reduce heat to medium-low, and cook for 10 minutes, or until the vegetables are fragrant and soft but not browned. Add the tomatoes. Increase heat to medium-high, stir, and cook another 3 minutes. Season with another pinch of salt and pepper. Add the red wine, chicken stock, fresh herb bundle, sugar, and chili pepper flakes. Bring to a boil over high heat, and then reduce to a simmer. Cook over medium or medium-low heat for 45 minutes, or until reduced by about one-third and thickened to a sauce-like consistency. Remove and discard herb bundle. Puree tomato sauce lightly with a hand-held immersion blender or in a stand blender for about 30 pulses, until frothy and chunky-smooth. Taste and adjust seasonings as necessary. Add the basil just before serving.

Sauce can be refrigerated for several days prior to using or frozen for up to 3 months.

TOMATES CONCASSEE

Less of a sauce than a chopping technique, these pretty little squares of tomato flesh can be tossed with a variety of seasonings, including garlic, scallions, shallots, olive oil, and fresh herbs, to form an instant fresh condiment for grilled or sautéed fish or to top toasted croutons as a kind of French bruschetta. Or they can be added to a finished sauce, such as Sauce Aurore (page 72) or Sauce Béarnaise (page 103).

To prepare *tomates concassee*, which means "crushed" or "ground" tomatoes, cut the outer flesh away from the peeled tomatoes with a paring knife. Work around the tomato, as you would if peeling a grapefruit. Discard the seed center and pulp. Stack the slices of tomato flesh and cut into petite strips about $1/8$ inch thick. Then cut the strips into a fine dice, producing tomato squares about $1/8$ inch.

SAUCE PUTTANESCA

(YIELD: 4 CUPS)

*The root of this sauce's name is saucy indeed (*putain *is French for "whore"), and it is likely so named due to its zesty, flavorful nature as well as how easily and quickly it comes together. Rife with black olives, capers, anchovies, hot chili pepper, fresh herbs and wine, it is scrumptious hot over pasta or accompanying fish—especially sturdy swordfish. It can also be served as a spread over toasted croutons with cocktails before dinner, either cold or at room temperature. Puttanesca can be stored in the refrigerator for a few days but doesn't freeze quite as well as the tomato sauce (page 118). It's not likely to last long anyway! Pay extra attention to salt flavoring, since many of the ingredients in this sauce are salty themselves.*

3 tablespoons extra virgin olive oil

3 large garlic cloves, minced

8 anchovy filets, coarsely chopped

6 medium tomatoes, peeled, seeded,
     and coarsely chopped

Pinch of sea salt or kosher salt

Freshly ground black pepper

3 tablespoons good-quality red wine

1/4 teaspoon red chili pepper flakes

2 tablespoons capers

1/2 cup pitted kalamata olives, thinly sliced

Generous pinch of granulated sugar

1/4 cup chopped fresh parsley leaves

1/4 cup chopped fresh basil leaves

In a large, deep skillet, heat the olive oil over medium-low heat. Add the garlic and anchovies. Cook gently, stirring, until the garlic has softened and the anchovies have become almost a paste, about 3 minutes. Add the tomatoes, a pinch of salt and pepper, wine, and chili flakes. Increase heat to medium-high and cook for 10 minutes, or until the tomatoes have cooked down and the wine has reduced into the sauce. Add the capers, olives, and sugar. Simmer over medium-low another 15 minutes, until the sauce has a thick, chunky consistency. Just before serving, add the chopped parsley and basil and stir through to heat. Taste and adjust seasonings as necessary. Serve immediately, or cool, refrigerate, and serve cold or reheated within 2 days.

SAUCE TOMATE "FORESTIÈRE"
Hunter's Tomato Sauce
(YIELD: 6 TO 7 CUPS)

A traditional sauce forestière *is largely composed of bacon and mushrooms. Its name derives from the mushrooms hunters would gather on their way back to their kitchens from "la chasse" (the hunt). As with a traditional forestière, the earthy nature of this sauce enhances pork, chicken, or quail. As a variation on a tomato sauce, it is also appetizing with pasta, especially a thicker, ridged noodle such as rigatoni.*

4 slices bacon, cut into small dice
Freshly ground black pepper
1 onion, finely chopped
2 garlic cloves, smashed and very finely chopped
4 cups finely sliced button mushrooms
Generous pinch of sea salt or kosher salt

1 cup good-quality red wine (e.g., Cabernet Sauvignon)
6 medium tomatoes, peeled, seeded, and coarsely chopped
1 cup chicken stock (page 24) or water
1 tablespoon finely chopped fresh rosemary
Pinch of granulated sugar

In a large pot or Dutch oven, cook the bacon, stirring, over medium-high heat until softened and most of the fat has been rendered, about 3 minutes. Season lightly with pepper. Reduce heat to medium. Add the onion and garlic, stirring. Cook 1 to 2 minutes, until just softened. Add the mushrooms, stir to coat, and season lightly with salt and pepper. Cook until wilted and softened, about 5 minutes. Add the wine, increase heat to medium-high, and boil lightly to reduce it by half. Add the tomatoes, stock or water, rosemary, and sugar. Bring to a simmer over high heat, and then reduce to low. Continue simmering until reduced by one-third, about 40 minutes. The consistency will be slightly chunky. Taste and adjust seasonings as needed. Serve immediately, or cool and store in the refrigerator for up to 3 days.

Le Théodore

Menu Gaspard à 23.50 €

(tous les jours midi et soir sauf le samedi)

entrées jour à 9.00 €

* Rémoulade de radis noir et céléri rave à la julienne de saumon fumé.
* Velouté crémeux de champignons frais aux éclats de noisettes grillées.
* Salade d'endives cuites marinées au citron.

Plats du jour à 13.50€

* Pavé de saumon vapeur à l'embeurrée de choux
* Tête de veau sauce Gribiche
* tranche de gigot d'agneau rôtie au piment.

Desserts jour à 8.50€

* Crumble aux pommes parfumé au Calvados
* Carpaccio d'oranges à la cannelle.

Acknowledgments

Extreme gratitude is extended to Gibbs Smith publishing and the amazing editorial and design team. Special thanks to editor Madge Baird, the brainchild of this book and series, and her special brand of personalized professionalism. Thanks to book designer Sheryl Dickert and production editor Melissa Dymock.

Without the support of my fabulous neighbors and taste-testers, along with my faithful canine kitchen companion and friend Tann Mann, this book couldn't have happened. Finally, thank you to France for inspiration "eternale."

Thanks to photographer Steven Rothfeld, chefs and culinary producers Claudia Sansone and Julie Logue-Riordan, and culinary assistant Rebecca Willis.

INDEX

METRIC CONVERSION CHART

Volume Measurements		Weight Measurements		Temperature Conversion	
U.S.	Metric	U.S.	Metric	Fahrenheit	Celsius
1 teaspoon	5 ml	1/2 ounce	15 g	250	120
1 tablespoon	15 ml	1 ounce	30 g	300	150
1/4 cup	60 ml	3 ounces	90 g	325	160
1/3 cup	75 ml	4 ounces	115 g	350	180
1/2 cup	125 ml	8 ounces	225 g	375	190
2/3 cup	150 ml	12 ounces	350 g	400	200
3/4 cup	175 ml	1 pound	450 g	425	220
1 cup	250 ml	2 1/4 pounds	1 kg	450	230